MW01635655

Mary Engelbreit Christmas Ideas

Meredith® Press
Des Moines, Iowa

Meredith® Press
An imprint of Meredith® Books

Mary Engelbreit: Christmas Ideas Make Good Cheer
Editor: Carol Field Dahlstrom
Technical Editor: Susan M. Banker
Graphic Designer: Angela Haupert Hoogensen
Copy and Production Editor: Terri Fredrickson
Contributing Copy Editor: Judith Stern Friedman
Contributing Proofreaders: Diane Doro, Jessica Kearney Heidgerken
Photographers: Andy Lyons Cameraworks, Scott Little
Technical Illustrator: Chris Neubauer Graphics, Inc.
Electronic Production Coordinator: Paula Forest
Editorial and Design Assistants: Judy Bailey, Mary Lee Gavin, Karen Schirm
Book Production Managers: Pam Kvitne, Marjorie J. Schenkelberg

Meredith® Books
Editor in Chief: James D. Blume
Design Director: Matt Strelecki
Managing Editor: Gregory H. Kayko

Director, Retail Sales and Marketing: Terry Unsworth
Director, Sales, Special Markets: Rita McMullen
Director, Sales, Premiums: Michael A. Peterson
Director, Sales, Retail: Tom Wierzbicki
Director, Book Marketing: Brad Elmitt
Director, Operations: George A. Susral
Director, Production: Douglas M. Johnston

Vice President, General Manager: Jamie L. Martin

Meredith Publishing Group
President, Publishing Group: Stephen M. Lacy
Vice President, Finance & Administration: Max Runciman

Meredith Corporation
Chairman and Chief Executive Officer: William T. Kerr

Chairman of the Executive Committee: E. T. Meredith III

All of us at Meredith® Press are dedicated to providing you with information and ideas to create beautiful and useful projects. We welcome your comments and suggestions. Write to us at: Meredith® Press, Crafts Editorial Department, 1716 Locust St., Des Moines, IA 50309-3023.

Printed in the United States of America.
ISBN: 0-696-22860-2
This edition published exclusively for Barnes & Noble, Inc. by Meredith Press.

Cover Illustration: Mary Engelbreit Studios

Isn't It Wonderful...

Homes are aglow with glistening lights reflecting off a blanket of powdery snow. Everyone I meet is humming a holiday tune, and I see twinkling in their eyes. Stores are dressed in their Christmas finery—showing off their holiday goodies. It must be Christmas!

There's no time quite like the holidays. It's a special time when we celebrate everywhere we go—decorating our homes and our hearts, filling them with the magic of the season.

One of my wishes this year is to share some of my special holiday designs with you. Every Christmas project in this book was inspired by one of my greeting card illustrations. You'll find dozens of ideas and treasures you can make to share with those you love.

From charming holiday ornaments and heirloom Christmas stockings to jolly, life-size snowmen to place out by the front evergreen and little girl dolls to make, you'll discover a sleigh-load of holiday fun in each of these five chapters.

Merry Christmas to you and your family. May the memories of this Christmas always shine bright.

Mary Engelbreit

CONTENTS

Have yourself a merry little Christmas, beginning with these wonderful projects inspired by Mary Engelbreit! Make them for your own holiday home or by the dozens to share during this glorious season of giving.

Merry Christmas Trims

Decking your house out for the holidays will be "Maryer" than ever with these festive decorations to make and treasure.

Center of Attention

Celebrate the spirit of Christmas with fun-to-do projects that shine both indoors and out.

Gifts from the Heart

No matter what type of crafting you like to do, Mary Engelbreit will inspire you to create wonderful projects to share during the season of giving.

All Dressed Up

Whether you want to treat yourself or a loved one to a holiday outfit or trim your front door for the season, you'll find all the ideas you need in this chapter.

Toys and Treasures

Fill their hearts with the magic only Christmas brings—cross-stitch a santa, paint a wood duck, crochet a loveable doll...all this and more awaits!

MERRY CHRISTMAS TRIMS

Your heart will be merry, merry, merry as you create these festive trims for your holiday home all inspired by Mary's holiday motifs. From charming ornaments to keepsake cross-stitch chair covers, the projects in this chapter are sure to stir the Christmas spirit.

CLAY CREATIONS

Brighten the branches of your evergreen with these easy-to-shape clay ornaments.

WHAT YOU'LL NEED
for one set

Rolling pin; polymer clay, such as Sculpey, in gingerbread brown, hot pink, white, red, green, black, and yellow
Gingerbread-man cookie cutter
1-inch eye pins; fine wire
Large seed beads in white and red
3-inch round cookie cutter
Tracing paper; pencil; scissors
Crafts knife; baking dish; ruler
Light green acrylic paint
Small paintbrush
2½-inch round cookie cutter
Two 5-inch-long pieces of copper crafting wire
Thick white crafts glue

HERE'S HOW

Gingerbread man

1 On a hard, smooth work surface, roll out gingerbread brown clay until it is approximately ¼-inch thick. Cut out a gingerbread man shape using a cookie cutter.

2 To create pink clay for cheeks, mix equal parts of hot pink and gingerbread brown clay together. Make two pea-sized circles. Press onto the cheek areas, using the diagram on *page 10* for placement.

3 Roll a 1⁄16-inch-wide strip of white clay by rolling with fingers on a smooth surface. Press strip down on gingerbread man in a wavy line to trim collar, hands, and feet as shown, *opposite.*

4 Roll black clay into tiny black balls for eyes, nose, and mouth. Press into place.

5 Roll three tiny red clay balls, and flatten them onto the front of the gingerbread man for buttons. Roll three tiny white clay balls, half the size of the red, and press onto the center of the red flowers. Shape six tiny green leaves, then add one on each side of the flowers. Shape a tiny green bow for hanger. Poke a hole through the center for stringing. Remove the wire.

6 Into the end of each hand, insert a small eye pin. Bake in oven according to product directions. Let cool.

7 Insert wire into one eye pin. String on red and white beads. Halfway through wire, add green bow. Finish stringing beads, and attach to the other end.

Wreath

1 Roll out green clay to about ¼-inch thick. Use a cookie cutter to cut out a doughnut shape about 3 inches in diameter.

2 Trace the leaf pattern, *page 11,* onto paper, and cut it out. Use the pattern to cut several leaves using a crafts knife. Make veins in each leaf by gently pressing a knife blade into the clay. Arrange leaves on the circle, overlapping as needed. Pinch and curve up the edges.

3 Roll several small red clay balls for berries. Press onto wreath where desired.

4 Roll out red clay to approximately ⅛-inch thick. For bow, cut two rectangles, one 2×1¼ inches, and the other 3×1½ inches. Lay the smaller rectangle centered on the larger one. Pinch the sides together in the middle to make a bow.

5 Roll another piece of red clay into a tubular shape about 1½ inches long. Flatten it, and wrap it around the center of the bow to make a band. Gently press the bow onto the wreath. Pierce two holes in the top of the bow for hanging.

6 Bake in the oven according to the product directions. Let cool.

7 Highlight the leaves using a small amount of light green paint, brushing gently over the raised areas.

8 Insert a 10-inch length of fine wire into one hole. Wrap the tail of the wire around itself to secure the end. String on beads, alternating red and white. Insert the tail of the wire through the opposite hole in the bow. Wrap the wire around itself to secure.

Teapot and Cup

1 Roll out yellow clay to approximately ¼-inch thick. Use a round cookie cutter to cut out a circle. Roll a small coil for the edge at the bottom of the pot. Trim away the excess clay.

2 For the spout, use the photograph, *opposite,* and the pattern on *page 11* as guides. Cut out a rectangle about ½×1½ inches. Angle one end. Attach to the pot by smoothing the clay together at the seam.

3 Roll a piece of red clay into a tubular shape about ⅛-inch thick. Use it to trim the teapot top and to make a separation between the lid and the base. Also trim the end of the spout. Trim away any excess clay. Insert an eye pin at the spout and over the handle area for the hanger.

4 To make the cup, cut out a circle about 1 inch in diameter. Cut off the top of the circle. Add a small rim on the bottom, the same as on the teapot base. Roll larger coils of red to shape handles for both the teapot and the cup. Press the handles into place. To attach the cup, coil two 5-inch pieces of copper wire around a pencil. Remove from pencil. Poke the ends into the spout and teacup as shown.

5 To add flowers, roll small balls from red clay. Add tiny white centers. Form V-shape leaves from green clay. Press into place.

6 Carefully place the clay pieces on a baking dish. Bake in the oven according to product directions. Let cool. Add a beaded hanger as on gingerbread man. Add glue to secure the wires if needed. Let the glue dry.

Tips for using polymer clay

- To avoid fingerprints showing on the clay, gently rub the surface back and forth before baking.
- Store leftover clay in a well-sealed, airtight plastic bag.
- When using cookie cutters to cut shapes from clay, choose cutters that are open, without a top and handle. The clay then can be gently pushed out of the cutter.
- To create uniform clay balls quickly, form a coil first, then cut off desired amounts. Roll the clay pieces into balls.
- To make holes in clay before baking, use an ice pick, paper clip, wire, or safety pin.
- When rolled thin enough, most polymer clay can be cut with regular or decorative-edge scissors.
- Cover the work surface with waxed paper before beginning to work with clay. The clay will pull away from the surface easily and will not discolor as it would if using newspaper. You also can use an old ceramic tile for your work surface.
- After working with clay, wash cookie cutters and baking dishes extremely well before using with food. Or, start a separate collection of cutters and dishes to be used only for craft projects.

GINGERBREAD ORNAMENT PLACEMENT GUIDE

TEAPOT AND CUP ORNAMENT
PLACEMENT GUIDE

WREATH ORNAMENT PATTERN

GARLAND OF GIFTS

These miniature packages are created from purchased wood blocks and brightly painted to deck the Christmas evergreen.

WHAT YOU'LL NEED

1-inch wood blocks
Drill with 1/8-inch bit
Sandpaper
Tack cloth
5/8-inch round wood beads
White spray primer, such as KILZ
Wood skewer
Acrylic paints in pink, white, lavender, sky blue, lime green, yellow, red, black, medium blue, and grass green
Medium flat paintbrush
Fine liner paintbrush
1/8-inch-wide red ribbon
Thick white crafts glue
Black pony beads
Cord

HERE'S HOW

1 Drill a hole through the center of each block. Sand if needed. Wipe away dust using a tack cloth.

2 In a well-ventilated work area, spray the blocks and wood beads lightly with white spray primer. Let dry. To paint several beads at once, stack them on a skewer. Lay the bead-filled skewer on paper, and paint all at once with a medium flat paintbrush. Let dry. Add white dots by dipping the handle end of a paintbrush into white paint and dotting onto the surface of the beads. Let the paint dry.

3 Paint each block a solid color. Let the paint dry. Use a fine liner brush to add small shapes, straight lines, wavy lines, bold stripes, or other desired designs. Our blocks have dark green lines on lime green, blue lines on lavender, red flowers on yellow, blue dots on light blue, red hearts on pink, and green hearts and dots on lime green. Let the paint dry.

4 Wrap red ribbon around each package, tying a bow at the top. Reinforce with small dots of glue if desired.

5 String the packages, painted beads, and black beads onto the desired length of cord. Knot each end.

ROCKIN' PONY

Complete with engaging details, this spotted pony ornament is reminiscent of a ready-to-ride childhood toy of yesteryear.

WHAT YOU'LL NEED
Tracing paper
Pencil
6×8-inch piece of ¼-inch thick wood; jigsaw or scroll saw
Fine sandpaper
Tack cloth
Sanding sealer
Paintbrush
Acrylic paints in red, black, white, and brown
Disposable foam plate
Natural sponge for painting
Scrap of bright blue felt
Scissors
Thick white crafts glue
Leather lacing in red and orange
Jute
2 gold beads
10-inch long pieces of wire in black and white; needle; thread
Scrap of red paper; paper punch
1¼×1¼-inch piece of heavy white paper
Fine black marking pen
2-inch long pieces of wire in white and green

HERE'S HOW

1 Trace the patterns, *below.* Transfer the pony pattern to a wood piece. Cut out around pony outline. To cut out shape between legs, first drill a hole to insert saw blade. Cut out the shape.

2 Lightly sand the wood shape. Remove dust using a tack cloth. Apply a coat of sealer. Let dry.

3 Paint the rocker red. While the paint is wet, outline in black, blending into the red. Let dry.

4 Place small amounts of white and black paint on a foam plate. Dampen the sponge with water. Dab sponge into the white and black paints. Dab off on plate. Sponge-paint the horse as desired. Let dry. Paint the hooves brown. Use a small paintbrush to add black outlines, eyes, and spots. Mix a little black and white to paint the inside of the ears grey. Let dry.

5 Use the saddle pattern to cut two sides from blue felt. Cut a 3/16-inch strip for saddle top. Glue to horse as shown on pattern. Paint a white highlight to each side of the saddle. Let dry.

6 Cut a 1¼-inch-long piece from orange lacing. Glue around horse's belly, from saddle bottom to saddle bottom. Cut two 1-inch pieces and one 4-inch piece from red lacing. Glue long piece as shown, from saddle, around nose, to other side of saddle. Glue a short piece of lacing on each side of horse's head as shown. Let dry.

7 Cut ½-inch-long pieces of jute for the horse's mane and 1-inch pieces for the tail. Glue in place. Let dry. Glue a

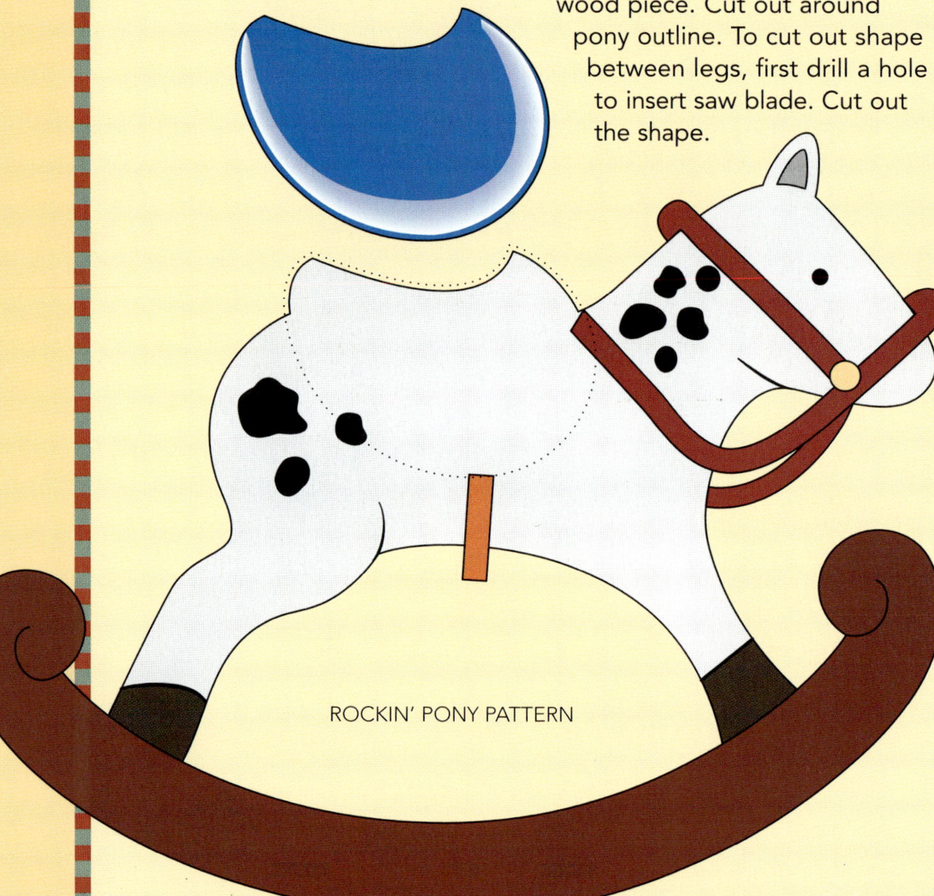
ROCKIN' PONY PATTERN

gold bead where red strips of lacing meet. Let dry.

8 Twist black and white wires together. Twist ends together to make a ring. Stitch to top of saddle for a hanger.

9 Cut a ⅛-inch-wide strip from red paper. Cut twenty ⅛-inch squares from strip. Glue squares around edge of white paper square, six on each side. Let dry. Punch a hole on one side. Write "For a Good Boy!" or other desired message on tag.

10 Twist short green and white wires together. Thread through hole in paper tag, and loop the tag around the horse's front leg.

From Santa

WRAPPED-UP-TIGHT ORNAMENTS

These dainty cross-stitched holiday packages, just like those on Mary's card, are complete with a mini tag from Santa himself.

WHAT YOU'LL NEED

One sheet of 14-count perforated plastic
Cotton embroidery floss in colors listed in key
Needle
1 yard of desired ribbon for bow
Metallic gold thread

HERE'S HOW

1 To make a package, you will need to stitch the design six times to make six sides. DO NOT cut the perforated plastic until all stitching is completed. To be sure all six sides fit on one piece of plastic, start in one corner, six holes in from the edges. Leave at least six holes between each design. Work the tag in the same manner.

2 Use two plies of cotton embroidery floss to work the cross-stitches over one square of plastic. Work the backstitches using one ply.

3 Using small, sharp scissors, carefully trim each stitched piece one square beyond the stitching on each side.

4 Using matching floss, whipstitch the edges of the star pieces together, forming a box. Tie the miniature packages with ribbon bows. Attach the tag around the ribbon bow using gold thread.

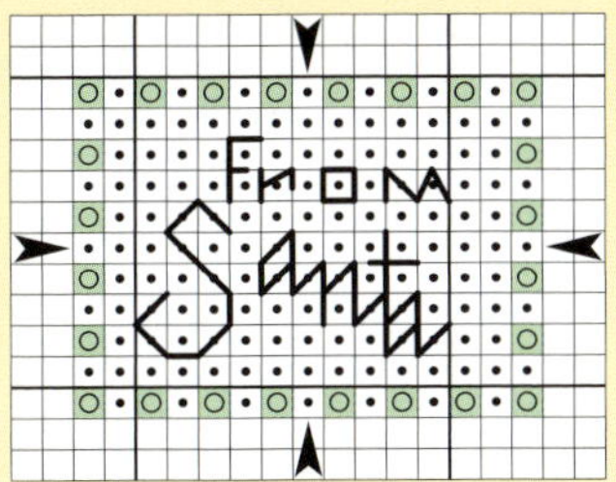

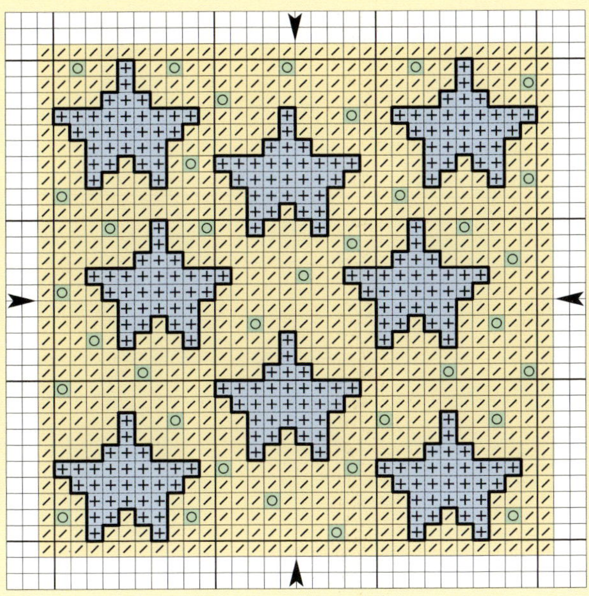

WRAPPED-UP-TIGHT ORNAMENTS

Anchor		DMC
002	•	000 White
257	O	703 Chartreuse
295	/	726 Topaz
159	+	3841 Baby blue

BACKSTITCH

403	/	310 Black – all stitches

Box sides stitch count: *32 high x 32 wide*

Box sides finished design sizes:
14-count fabric – 2¼ x 2¼ inches
16-count fabric – 2 x 2 inches
18-count fabric – 1¾ x 1¾ inches

Gift tag stitch count: *11 high x 15 wide*

Gift tag finished design sizes:
14-count fabric – ⅞ x 1 inch
16-count fabric – ⅝ x 1 inch
18-count fabric – ⅝ x ⅞ inch

FAVORITE TOYS SEAT COVER

You'll find yourself reminiscing about childhood toys and treasures when you admire this stunning seat cover stitched on rich black fabric.

WHAT YOU'LL NEED

24×24-inch piece of 28-count black Jobelan fabric
Cotton embroidery floss in colors listed in key, pages 22–23
Needle
24×24-inch piece of fleece or batting
1½ yards of red sew-in piping
Staple gun and staples
Child's chair appropriate for a seat cover

HERE'S HOW

1 Tape or zigzag the edges of the fabric to prevent fraying. Find the center of the chart and the center of the fabric; begin stitching there.

2 Use two plies of floss to work the cross-stitches over two threads of fabric. Work the backstitches, straight stitches, and satin stitches as indicated in the key, using the diagrams on *pages 190–191* as a guide. Use two plies of floss to work the French knots, *page 190.*

3 To finish the seat cover, you may want to take your stitched piece to a professional upholsterer. To cover a chair like ours, add fleece or batting to the wood chair seat, stapling the edge to the back side. Center the stitched design over the batting. Staple to the back side of the chair, folding and mitering the extra fabric at the corners. Trim the edge of the cushion with piping by stapling to the back side.

FAVORITE TOYS SEAT COVER *continued*

FAVORITE TOYS SEAT COVER *continued*

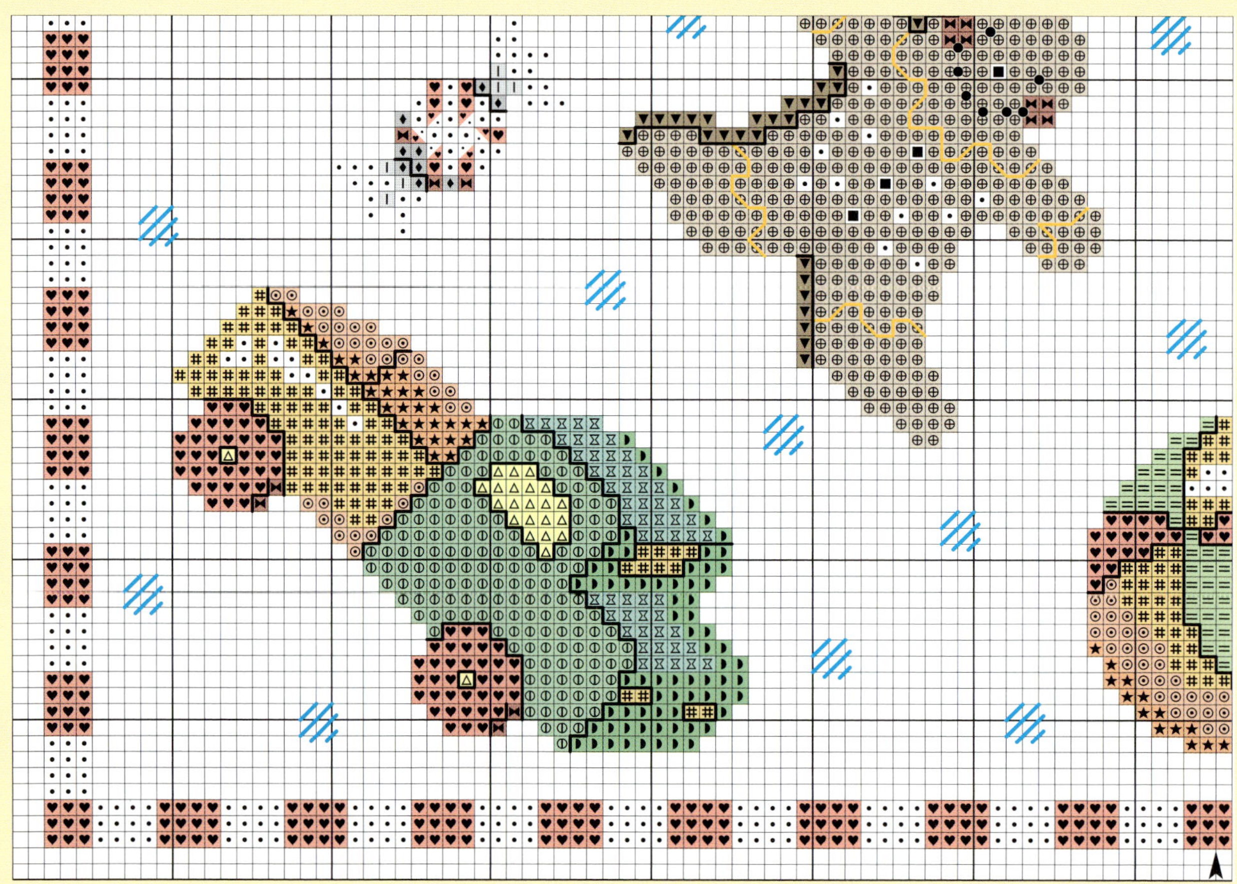

Anchor	DMC
002	000 White
403	310 Black
1018	316 Antique mauve
235	414 Steel
398	415 Pearl gray
374	420 Medium hazel
1005	498 Christmas red
059	600 Deep cranberry
062	603 True cranberry
075	604 Light cranberry
392	642 Medium beige-gray
391	644 Light beige-gray
326	720 Bittersweet
304	741 Tangerine

Anchor	DMC
023	818 Pink
146	827 Powder blue
897	902 Garnet
255	907 Light parrot green
298	972 Deep canary
297	973 True canary
244	987 Forest green
410	995 Dark electric blue
433	996 Light electric blue
397	3072 Beaver gray
1050	3781 Mocha
923	3818 Emerald
373	3828 True hazel
1074	3848 Teal-green

Anchor	DMC
BLENDED NEEDLE	
255 256	907 Light parrot green (1X) and 906 Medium parrot green (2X)
244 228	987 Forest green (1X) and 700 Christmas green (2X)
BACKSTITCH	
002	000 White – gingerbread man icing (3X); letter "P" (2X)
403	310 Black – all other stitches (1X)
1018	316 Antique mauve – teddy bear cheeks (1X)
1005	498 Christmas red – doll and soldier mouths (2X); cup's saucer (1X)

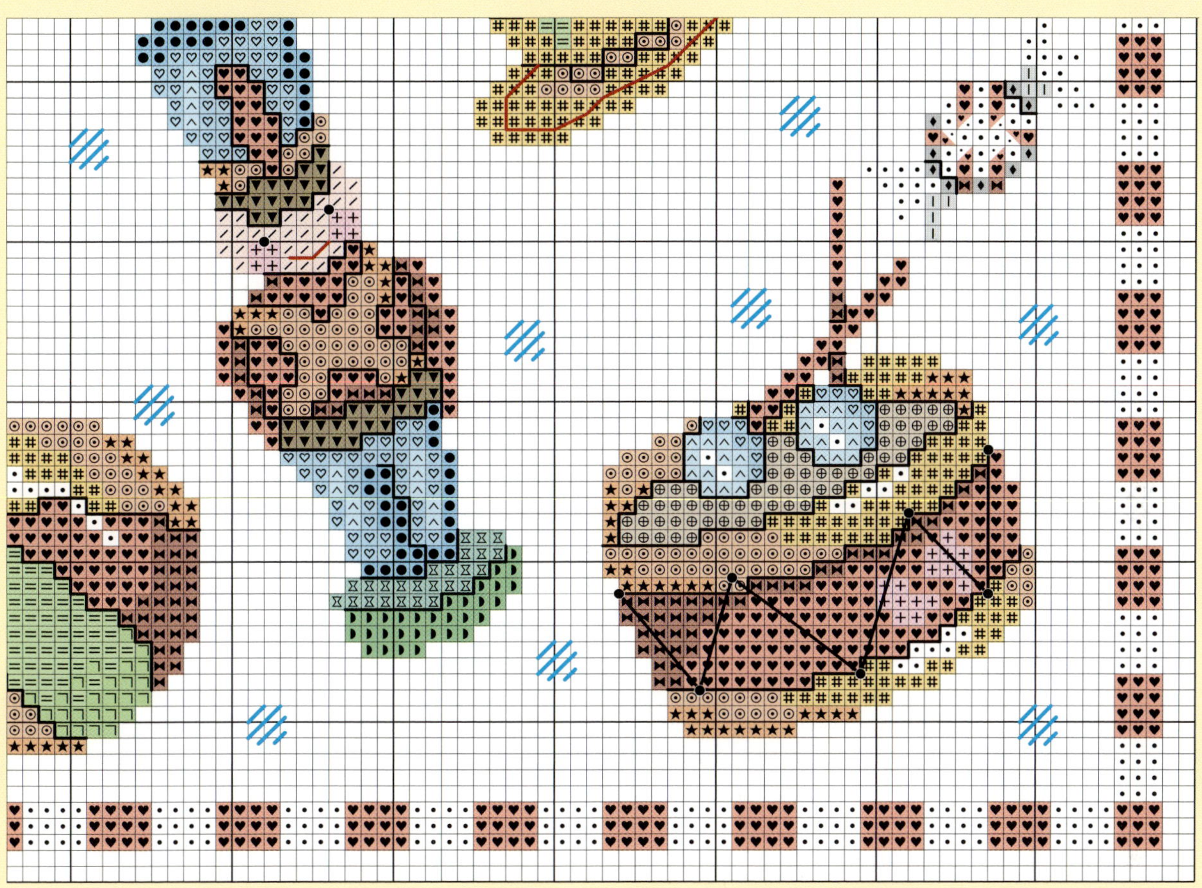

Anchor DMC
BACKSTITCH
059 600 Deep cranberry – doll's dress (2X)
257 905 Dark parrot green – bird's wing (2X)
256 906 Medium parrot green – teapot (1X)
244 987 Forest green – gift box (2X)
410 995 Dark electric blue – string for duck toy (3X)

Anchor DMC
STRAIGHT STITCH
403 310 Black – drum strings (2X)
SATIN STITCH
002 000 White – background (4X)
FRENCH KNOT
403 310 Black – eyes, drum, and gingerbread man mouth
298 972 Deep canary – wheels on duck toy
244 987 Forest green – gift box

Stitch count: *146 high x 146 wide*
Finished design sizes:
28-count fabric – 10½ x 10½ inches
32-count fabric – 9⅛ x 9⅛ inches
36-count fabric – 8⅛ x 8⅛ inches

YULETIDE TRIM

This free-spirited gingerbread man is made of wood and painted with one of Mary's cheerful illustrated expressions.

WHAT YOU'LL NEED

Tracing paper; pencil; scissors
8×10-inch piece of ½-inch pine
Small pieces of ¼-inch pine
Sandpaper; drill and small bit
Cloth; white spray primer
Acrylic paints in light warm brown, tan, white, light blue, red, peach, black, and yellow
Medium flat and fine liner paintbrushes; natural sponge
Three ½-inch wood plugs
Small wood ovals; wood glue
Red rickrack; wire; branch

HERE'S HOW

1 Enlarge and trace patterns, *below,* onto tracing paper. Cut out, and trace onto ½-inch-thick pine. Cut out all pieces and sand edges. Cut the tie and star out of ¼-inch pine.

YULETIDE TRIM PATTERN 1 SQUARE = 1 INCH

2 Drill a tiny hole in the star for a hanger. Drill holes in the sides of the hands for inserting a branch and wire.

3 Wipe off dust, and spray with white primer. Let dry.

4 Using a medium flat brush, paint the gingerbread man light warm brown.

5 To add texture, sponge on paint using a small natural sponge. Soak sponge with water first. Squeeze out excess water. Use a tan paint (lighter than the base color of the gingerbread man). Thin the paint with water to the consistency of light cream. You may want to sponge some paint off onto paper before painting on wood. Begin lightly sponging tan onto gingerbread man, starting in the center and fading out toward the edges. Let the paint dry.

6 To transfer the face pattern, color the back side of the face drawing using a soft lead pencil. Lay the pattern onto the round wood head with the right side up. Tape the pattern in place.

Using a sharp hard pencil, draw over the pattern lines to transfer the eyes, nose, mouth, and cheek lines onto the painted wood.

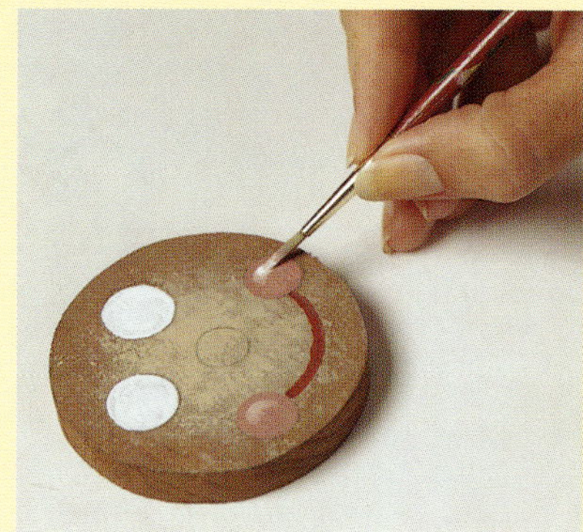

7 Paint round white eyes. Let dry. Add a crescent-shape light blue shadow in the upper right sides of eyes. Paint small black pupils. Let dry. Add tiny white dots to pupils. Outline eyes

and lashes in black. Paint the mouth red. Paint peach cheeks. While the peach paint is wet, highlight the upper right sides of cheeks with white. Let dry.

8 Use ½-inch wood plugs for the nose and the buttons. Paint the plugs red. Let dry. Add a tiny white comma-shape highlight to the nose. Paint white dots in the centers of remaining plugs. Paint the wood ovals green.

9 Paint the tie white. Let dry. Add wide and narrow red stripes as shown, *above*. Paint the star yellow and let dry.

10 Glue the wood pieces in place. Glue rickrack onto hands and feet. Let the glue dry.

11 Coil a piece of wire around a pencil and remove. Attach wire to star and to hand. Insert a branch into the other hand. Add glue to secure.

JING-A-LING GARLAND

WHAT YOU'LL NEED

Small metal bells (available at craft and discount stores)
Yellow spray paint
Enamel gloss paints in red, lime green, white, and orange
Small liner paintbrush
Rubber bands, optional

Ring out the joy of this glorious time of year with a garland of painted bells and bold wood beads.

Mineral spirits
½-inch-wide red satin ribbon
Fine string
Wood beads in black and white

HERE'S HOW

1 Spray-paint the bells yellow. Let the paint dry. Apply a second coat if necessary. Let dry.

2 Using the photograph, *above*, for inspiration, paint very simple lines and shapes using enamel paints. If painting straight lines, use rubber bands as guides. Let paint dry before removing bands. To paint dots or flowers, dip the eraser end of a pencil or a paintbrush handle into paint, and dot onto surface. If using two colors, let dry between coats. Clean the paintbrush with mineral spirits.

3 Cut ribbon into 12-inch lengths. Thread ribbon through bell tops, and tie into bows. Thread bells onto string, alternating black and white beads in between bells.

IT'S CHRISTMAS!

CUTE 'N' CLEVER CARD CADDY

Keep all of your holiday greeting cards organized and cleverly displayed in this adorable cross-stitched holder.

WHAT YOU'LL NEED

14×18-inch piece of 22-count white Janina fabric for pocket
26×18-inch piece of 22-count blue Janina fabric for background
Cotton embroidery floss in colors listed in key, pages 30–31
Twelve ¼-inch yellow star buttons
Seed beads as listed in key
Needle; embroidery hoop
½ yard of lining fabric
½ yard fleece
2 yards of sew-in red piping
16¼-inch piece of ¾-inch dowel
Two 2-inch wood stars
Two 1-inch wood finishing discs
Blue/gray acrylic paint; paintbrush
Spray acrylic varnish
Thick white crafts glue
Five ½-inch wood bells
⅛-inch black satin ribbon
1 white ½-inch pom-pom
1 yard of cord for hanging

HERE'S HOW

1 Tape or zigzag edges of the white Janina fabric to prevent fraying. Find the center of the pocket chart, *pages 30–31,* and the center of the fabric; begin stitching there. Use three plies of floss to work the cross-stitches over two threads of fabric. Work the French knots, *page 190,* using two plies of floss. Work the remaining stitches as indicated in the key. Sew on beads and buttons according to chart. Press the finished piece from the back.

2 Tape or zigzag edges of the blue Janina fabric to prevent fraying. Measure 10 inches in from the middle of one short end, and mark as the center for the background stitching. Find the center of the chart, *pages 32–33,* and the center marking on fabric; begin stitching there. Use three plies of floss to work cross-stitches over two threads of fabric. Work the remaining stitches as indicated in key. Sew on beads and buttons according to chart. Press from back.

3 Cut blue back-stitched piece to measure 13×20 inches, trimming the sides and bottom only, allowing 8½ inches of unstitched fabric below the design for the inside pocket.

4 Cut the pocket design to measure 13×8½ inches, with the top of the design ½ inch down from the top edge of the pocket. Cut the linings for the back and the pocket the same sizes as the cross-stitched pieces.

5 Stitch using a ½-inch seam allowance, with right sides facing. Line the pocket with fleece. Stitch piping across the top of the pocket. Stitch pocket lining on piping line. Trim away fleece from seam allowance. Trim seam. Press lining to wrong side. Baste raw edges even.

6 Line the back cross-stitch piece with fleece. Position the pocket even with cross-stitch back at lower edge. Pin or baste. Draw curved bottom corners of pocket onto fabric.

7 Starting at the top on one side of the back cross-stitch piece, stitch piping to back and pocket edge along bottom curve and up the opposite side. Stitch lining to back on piping line, leaving an opening for turning. Trim fleece; clip curve. Turn to right side. Lightly press.

8 Machine-zigzag or serge across top edge of design. Turn back 2 inches along the top edge. Hand-stitch to back side, creating a casing for the dowel.

9 Paint the dowel, stars, bells, and finishing discs. Let dry. Spray with acrylic varnish. Let dry.

10 Glue the finishing discs to the ends of the dowel. Slip the dowel into casing. Glue the stars to the front of the dowel and let dry.

11 Hand-stitch painted bells on black ribbon according to the photo. Glue a pom-pom to girl's hat. Tie a cord on the dowel for hanging.

CUTE 'N' CLEVER CARD CADDY *continued*

Anchor		DMC	Anchor		DMC	Anchor		DMC
002	•	000 White	858	○	524 Light olive drab	1022	⊕	760 Salmon
1006	□	304 Christmas red	898	◉	611 Drab brown	259	∨	772 Loden
403	■	310 Black	874	^	676 Light old gold	024	♡	776 Pink
370	☆	434 Medium chestnut	239	▽	702 Christmas green	1012	–	948 Light peach
1046	=	435 Light chestnut	256	‖	704 Chartreuse	242	∖	989 Forest green
233	♦	451 Shell gray	324	⧗	721 Bittersweet	391	∾	3033 Pale mocha
683	▲	500 Deep blue-green	295	◇	726 Topaz	1031	/	3753 Antique blue
875	⊡	503 True blue-green	891	×	729 Medium old gold	236	●	3799 Charcoal
862	★	520 Deep olive drab	303	△	742 Tangerine	877	✱	3815 Celadon green
860	∩	522 Dark olive drab	868	+	754 Medium peach	301	⌓	3822 Light straw

Anchor DMC

386 3823 Yellow
031 3833 Raspberry
410 3844 Dark bright turquoise
433 3846 Light bright turquoise
305 3852 Deep straw
926 3866 Light mocha

BLENDED NEEDLE

8581 646 Beaver gray (2X) and
233 451 Shell gray (1X)
236 3799 Charcoal (2X) and
400 317 Pewter (1X)
363 3827 Golden brown (2X) and
1045 436 Tan (1X)

HALF CROSS-STITCH
(stitch in direction of symbol)

295 726 Topaz – star glow

BACKSTITCH

002 000 White – gingerbread icing (2X); flowers on skirt (1X)

Anchor DMC

BACKSTITCH

1006 304 Christmas red – gingerbread mouths, ornaments, scarf, skirt, elf, gingerbread bow (2X)
403 310 Black – all other stitches
1046 435 Light chestnut – small gingerbread people (2X)
239 702 Christmas green – elf collar (2X); candy cane (1X)
295 726 Topaz – snowman's hat (1X)
242 989 Forest green – stars on elf's jacket (1X)
236 3799 Charcoal – tree branch needles, girl's boots and scarf (2X)

STRAIGHT STITCH

002 000 White – carrot highlight (2X)
236 3799 Charcoal – tree branch stems (3X)

Anchor DMC

FRENCH KNOT

1006 304 Christmas red – flowers on skirt, elf, snowman's hat
403 310 Black – snowman mouth, girl's jacket, gingerbread eyes, jingle bell of elf's hat
217 367 Pistachio – mittens

MILL HILL BEADS

00161 Crystal glass beads – elf and gingerbread sugar
02002 Yellow creme glass beads – garland on trees
02013 Red glass beads – buttons, trees, gingerbread people
02014 Black glass beads – buttons
Yellow stars – elf

CUTE 'N' CLEVER CARD CADDY *continued*

Back piece stitch count: *97 high x 132 wide*

Back piece finished design sizes:

22-count fabric – 8¾ x 12 inches

28-count fabric – 7 x 9½ inches

32-count fabric – 6 x 8¼ inches

Pocket stitch count: *77 high x 138 wide*

Pocket finished design sizes:

22-count fabric – 7 x 12½ inches

28-count fabric – 5½ x 9⅞ inches

32-count fabric – 4⅞ x 8⅝ inches

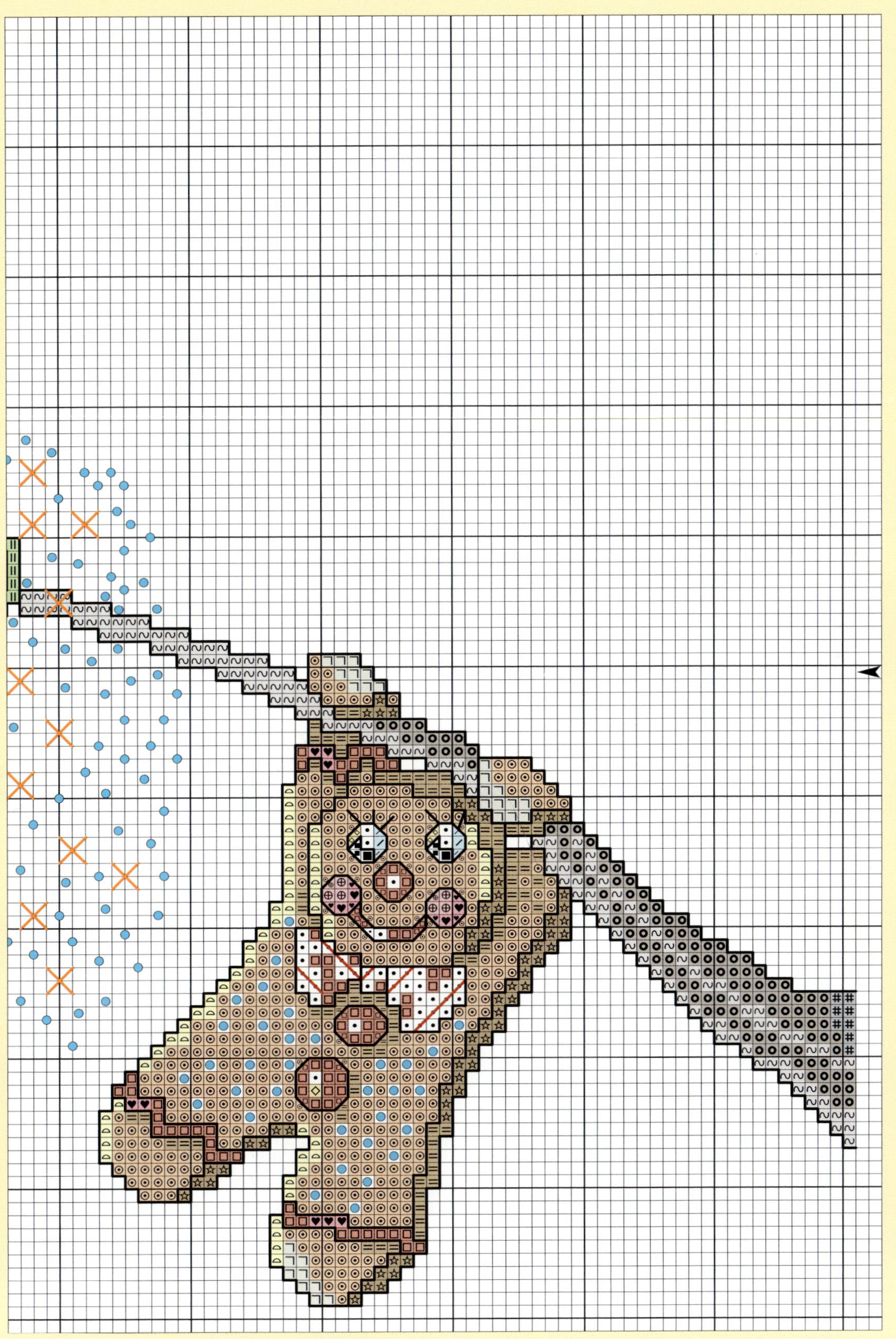

PRETTY MITTS

Sweet little patterns dance on these cross-stitched mitten ornaments. Turn the page for more of Mary's merry motifs.

WHAT YOU'LL NEED

10×10-inch piece of 28-count cream, white, teal, red, or gold color Lugana fabric
Cotton embroidery floss in colors listed in key
Needle; embroidery hoop
Tracing paper and pencil
Fabric marking pencil
6×6-inch piece of red felt
6×6-inch piece of lining fabric
8 inches of sew-in narrow piping
12-inch piece of ½-inch-wide red flat braid trim
Fabric glue; gold ring
½ yard of ribbon for trim

HERE'S HOW

1 Tape or zigzag edges of the Lugana fabric to prevent fraying. Find the center of the desired chart, *below or on pages 36–37*, and the center of the fabric; begin stitching there. Use two plies of floss to work the cross-stitches over two threads of fabric. Work the backstitches using one ply. Press the finished piece from the back.

2 Trace and cut out the mitten pattern. Trace the shape around the cross stitch. Machine-stitch along the line. Cut out the mitten, allowing a ¼-inch seam allowance. Cut the shape from felt and lining fabric.

3 Stitch piping across the top of the cross-stitch, close to the design, leaving an equal amount of piping for stitching to felt back piece. With right sides facing, stitch lining to mitten along piping. Turn to right side, and baste together on machine stitching line. Trim seam from top of felt mitten shape.

4 Stitch felt shape to remainder of piping with thumbs at opposite sides. Place mitten shapes together, wrong sides facing. Top-stitch through all layers on machine stitching. Trim seam allowance close to stitching. Glue trim over seam. Add gold ring at top. Thread ribbon through ring, and tie into a bow.

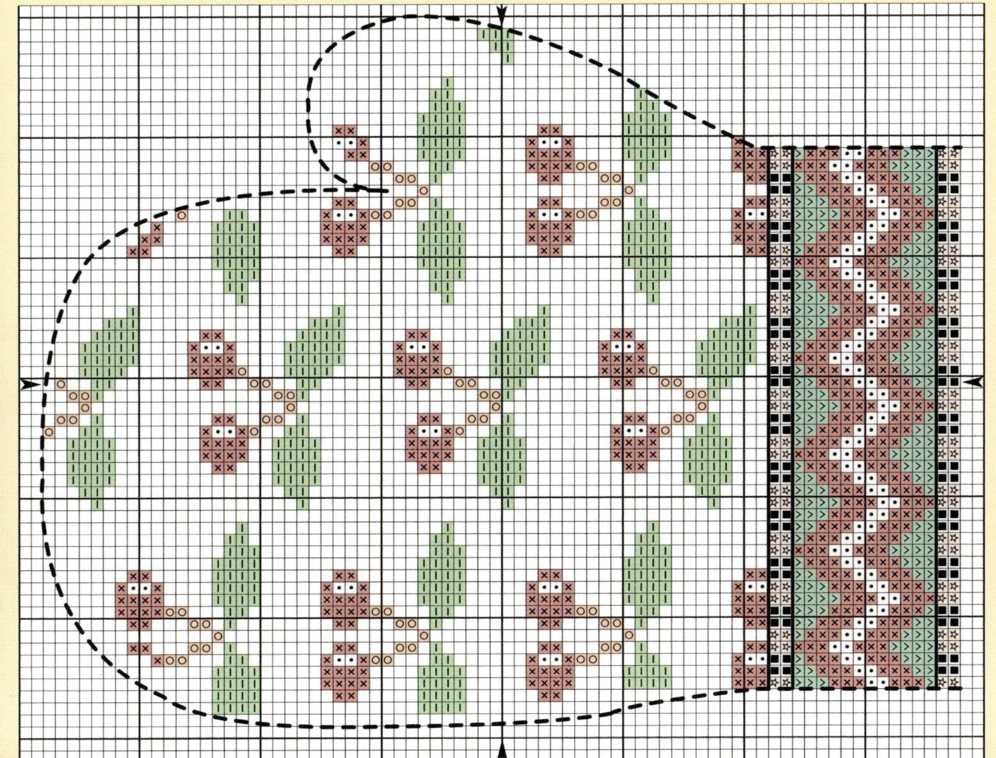

Teal Mitten stitch count:
76 high x 57 wide
Teal Mitten finished design sizes:
28-count fabric – 5½ x 4 inches
32-count fabric – 4¾ x 3½ inches
36-count fabric – 4¼ x 3⅛ inches

Anchor	Symbol	DMC
002	•	000 White
290	□	307 Lemon
403	■	310 Black
9046	×	321 Christmas red
256	–	704 Chartreuse
9575	○	758 Terra-cotta
1010	☆	951 Ivory
298	◉	972 Canary
1044	♡	3345 Medium hunter green
268	^	3346 Light hunter green
164	♦	3842 Wedgwood
BACKSTITCH		
002	/	000 White – white mitten (2X)
403	/	310 Black – mitten cuffs (2X)

MITTS *continued*

Red Mitten stitch count: *76 high x 57 wide*
Red Mitten finished design sizes:
28-count fabric – 5½ x 4 inches
32-count fabric – 4¾ x 3½ inches
36-count fabric – 4¼ x 3⅛ inches

White Mitten stitch count: *76 high x 59 wide*
White Mitten finished design sizes:
28-count fabric – 5½ x 4¼ inches
32-count fabric – 4¾ x 3⅝ inches
36-count fabric – 4¼ x 3¼ inches

Gold Mitten stitch count: *76 high x 58 wide*
Gold Mitten finished design sizes:
28-count fabric – 5½ x 4⅛ inches
32-count fabric – 4¾ x 3⅝ inches
36-count fabric – 4¼ x 3¼ inches

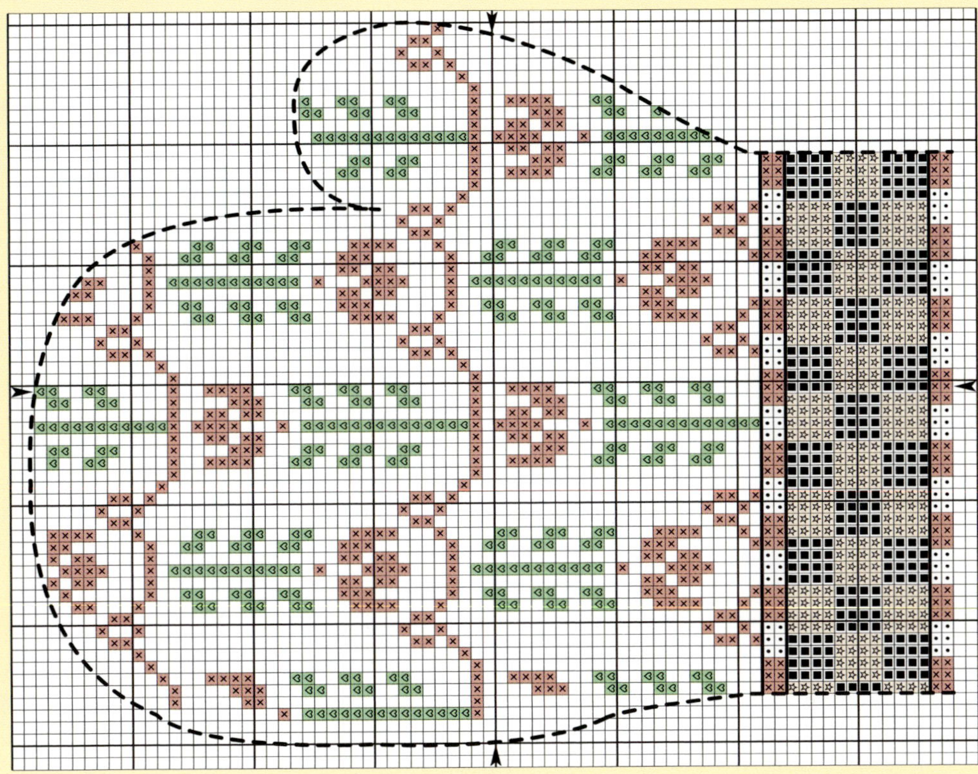

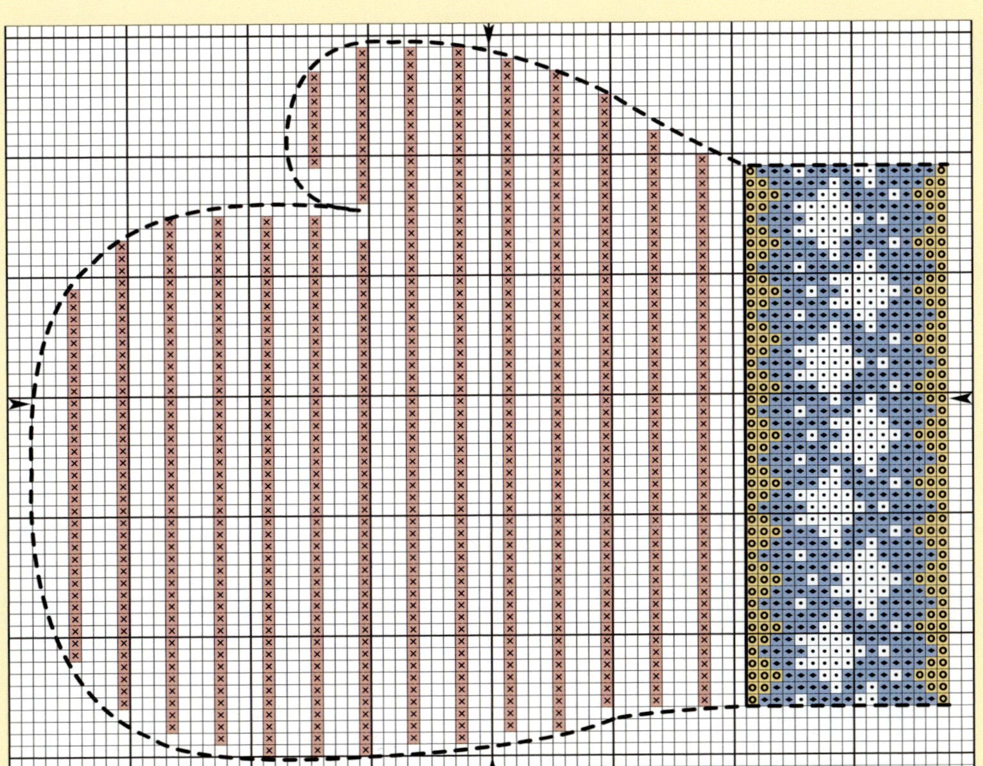

Cream Mitten stitch count: *73 high x 59 wide*
Cream Mitten finished design sizes:
28-count fabric – 5¼ x 4¼ inches
32-count fabric – 4½ x 3⅝ inches
36-count fabric – 4 x 3¼ inches

We Wish You A Very
Merry Christmas

SNOW PALS SAMPLER

Accented with beads, chenille stems, and star sequins, this cross-stitched version of Mary's Santa and the Snowboys comes alive with sparkle and dimension. The key is below. Instructions and chart begin on page 40.

Anchor	DMC
1025	347 Deep salmon
217	367 Pistachio
371	433 Dark chestnut
1045	436 Tan
817	469 Avocado
683	500 Blue-green
874	676 Light old gold
885	677 Pale old gold
890	680 Dark old gold
256	704 Chartreuse
326	720 Bittersweet
293	727 Pale topaz
302	743 Yellow
1022	760 True salmon
144	800 Delft blue
140	813 Powder blue
043	815 Medium garnet
897	902 Deep garnet
4146	950 Rose-beige
1010	951 Ivory
243	988 Forest green
905	3021 Brown-gray
1024	3328 Dark salmon
267	3362 Loden
1088	3790 Beige-gray
306	3820 Dark straw
305	3821 True straw
410	3844 Dark bright turquoise
324	3853 Dark autumn gold
001	3865 Winter white

BLENDED NEEDLE

Anchor	DMC
150 133	336 Navy (2X) and 796 Royal blue (1X)
1025 1006	347 Deep salmon (2X) and 304 Christmas red (1X)
855 891	370 Pecan (2X) and 729 Medium old gold (1X)
302 297	743 Yellow (2X) and 973 Canary (1X)
275 1046	780 Deep topaz (2X) and 435 Light chestnut (1X)
433 167	996 Electric blue (2X) and 3766 Peacock blue (1X)
433 186	996 Electric blue (2X) and 3846 Light bright turquoise (1X)
1024 1022	3328 Dark salmon (2X) and 760 True salmon (1X)
1020 4146	3713 Pale salmon (2X) and 950 Rose-beige (1X)
167 433	3766 Peacock blue (2X) and 996 Electric blue (1X)
363 305	3827 Golden brown (2X) and 3821 True straw (1X)
159 1060	3841 Baby blue (2X) and 747 Sky blue (1X)
313 303	3854 Medium autumn gold (2X) and 742 Tangerine (1X)
306 324 303	3820 Dark straw (1X) and 3853 Dark autumn gold (1X) and 742 Tangerine (1X)

BACKSTITCH

Anchor	DMC
403	310 Black – all other stitches (1X)
1025	347 Deep salmon – cape detail, basket (2X); scarf, horse, ornament with bow, ribbon, Santa's mouth and hat, candy, and train (1X)
217	367 Pistachio – scarf (2X); gift box, tree stand, train window, and ornament (1X)
371	433 Dark chestnut – basket (1X); branches (3X)
817	469 Avocado – top of train (1X)
256	704 Chartreuse – holly (1X)
326	720 Bittersweet – stars, hat, and ornament (1X)
293	727 Pale topaz – ornament, hat, moon, top of snowman's head (1X)
302	743 Yellow – lettering (4X)
1089	3845 Medium bright turquoise – scarf (1X); snowman outline (2X)
324	3853 Dark autumn gold – lettering (4X)
001	3865 Winter white – train window, ball under tree (1X); tree detail (2X); lettering (4X)

STRAIGHT STITCH

Anchor	DMC
403	310 Black – button detail (1X)
1025	347 Deep salmon – ornament base (2X)
326	720 Bittersweet – ornament base (2X)
303	742 Tangerine – scarf fringe (3X)
1022	760 True salmon – horse's ear and rocker (2X); berries, scarf (1X)
1041	844 Beaver gray – fur detail on Santa, eyelashes on snowman, teddy bear, and tree garland
243	988 Forest green – scarf (2X)
1089	3845 Medium bright turquoise – train wheels, inside basket (1X)
001	3865 Winter white – stars on snowman's hat, pom-pom on Santa's hat, garland on tree (2X)

FRENCH KNOT

Anchor	DMC
002	000 White – top of basket
403	310 Black – eyes, buttons, rocking horse, tree
1025	347 Deep salmon – cape, ornament, train wheels
217	367 Pistachio – scarf
1089	3845 Medium bright turquoise – scarf
313	3854 Medium autumn gold – teddy bear
001	3865 Winter white – lettering

SURFACE EMBELLISHMENTS

- Sequin gold stars with seed bead – basket trim
- Large gold seed beads – basket trim
- White bugle beads – ear muffs
- Red bugle beads – ear muffs
- Gold bugle beads with small beads – garland
- Green chenille stems – snowman's hat and ear muffs
- Red chenille stems – snowman's hat

Stitch count: *203 high x 144 wide*

Finished design sizes:
28-count fabric – 14½ x 10¼ inches
32-count fabric – 12⅝ x 9 inches
36-count fabric – 11¼ x 8 inches

SNOW PALS SAMPLER *continued*

WHAT YOU'LL NEED

24×20-inch piece of 28-count black Jobelan fabric
Cotton embroidery floss in colors listed in key, page 39
Needle
Embroidery hoop
Surface embellishments as listed in key
Beading needle
Matching thread
Desired mat and frame

HERE'S HOW

1 Tape or zigzag edges of the Jobelan fabric to prevent fraying. Find the center of the chart, *pages 42–43*, and the center of the fabric; begin

stitching there. Use two plies of floss to work the cross-stitches over two threads of fabric. Work the French knots, *page 190*, using two plies. Work the other stitches as indicated in the key.

2 Press the finished piece from the back. Attach the beads using one ply of matching floss. Cut pieces of chenille stems to appropriate lengths. Tack into place using couching stitches.

3 Mat and frame the stitched piece as desired.

OH-SO-MERRY TOPIARY

Just the right size for a holiday centerpiece, this everlasting topiary is planted in a brightly painted flowerpot.

WHAT YOU'LL NEED

12-inch-high plastic foam cone, such as Styrofoam
Thick white crafts glue
14×18- and 8×8-inch pieces of dark green felt
Straight pins
Scissors
Tracing paper
Pencil
White rickrack
White pom-pom garland
Wood star
Acrylic paints in green, yellow, and red
Paintbrush
Drill and small drill bit
Wire
Small scraps of light green felt
Red thumb tacks
Stick
Small flowerpot
Plastic foam, such as Styrofoam, to fit in pot
White shredded paper

HERE'S HOW

1 Coat the foam cone with glue. Lay the cone on the large piece of dark green felt. Line up the short edge of the felt vertically on the cone. Pin the edge in place. Shape the felt around the cone until covered. Trim off the extra felt. Pin felt in place until the glue dries. Remove the pins.

2 Place the cone on another piece of dark green felt. Cut out a circle that is 1½ inches larger all the way around the bottom of the foam cone. Cut a small hole in the center of the circle for inserting the stick.

3 Glue a piece of large white rickrack around the edge of the circle. Glue the circle onto the bottom of the felt-covered cone, rickrack side up. Let the glue dry. Pin one end of the garland at the top of the tree. Wrap the garland around the tree as shown, *opposite*, pinning to secure.

4 Paint the star yellow. Let it dry. Drill a small hole in the bottom of the star, attach wire, then insert wired star into the top of the tree.

5 Trace the leaf pattern, *right*. Cut out. Use pattern to cut small green leaves from felt. Push red tacks through the center of the leaves, then into the tree. Add a dot of yellow paint in the center of each flower by dipping the handle end of a small paintbrush into paint, and dotting onto the tack.

6 Insert a stick into the bottom of the finished tree, through the felt, and into the cone far enough to hold it sturdily.

7 Paint the flowerpot yellow. Let it dry. Add red and green stripes as shown, *opposite*. Let the paint dry.

8 Insert a piece of foam into the pot so it fits snugly. Reinforce with glue if needed. Push tree stick into the center of the pot. Fill the top of the pot with white shredded paper.

FLOWER AND LEAF PATTERNS

S
C
ME

Center of Attention

Add star attractions throughout your home with festive accents that shout "celebration!" You'll find a jolly elf to brighten the yard, keepsake stockings and frames that magnify the mantel, and many more clever ideas that all reflect Mary's charm and whimsy.

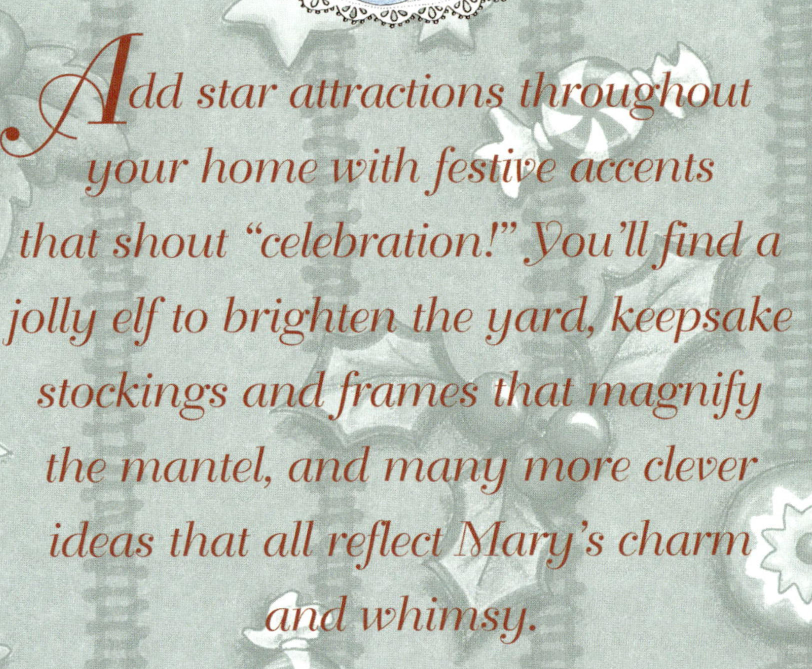

WHITE-AS-SNOW DOILY

Made from white linen, this delicate doily is edged with an elegant crocheted accent.

WHAT YOU'LL NEED

Pencil; tissue paper; straight pins
14×14-inch piece of white linen
White rayon machine embroidery thread; small scissors
14×14-inch piece of tear-away fabric stabilizer; #3 crochet hook
Large-eyed sewing needle
One skein of #8 white pearl cotton
Two skeins of #5 white pearl cotton

HERE'S HOW

1 Enlarge and trace pattern, *below,* onto tissue paper. Pin paper pattern onto linen fabric.

2 Machine-stitch on traced outside line and on cutouts. Use small scissors to cut out doily close to stitching around outside edge, and around cutouts on inside edge.

WHITE-AS-SNOW DOILY PATTERN 1 SQUARE = 1 INCH

3 Using fabric stabilizer, machine-satin-stitch with rayon thread around the cutouts. Hand press ⅛-inch of raw edge to wrong side. Using a needle and #8 pearl cotton, work blanket stitches around the outside edge, with stitches a scant ¼ inch apart. (See *page 190*.)

4 Alternate bobble and slip stitches around outside edge using #5 pearl cotton and the crochet hook.

With the RS facing, join cotton in any blanket stitch space along edge with a slip stitch, ch 2.

* Step 1: yo hook, insert the hook into the same blanket stitch space, yo hook and draw through the first two lps on the hook.
Step 2: working into the same blanket stitch space, repeat Step 1 until there are four lps on the hook, yo hook and draw through all four lps. Ch 1, sl st into same blanket stitch space to complete one bobble.
Step 3: sl st in each of the next 3 blanket stitch spaces. In next blanket stitch space, sl st, ch 2. Rep from * around outer edge ending sl st in beginning space. Fasten off.

5 Work a machine decorative stitch on the inner circle where indicated on pattern.

Note: The crochet abbreviations are on page 191.

THE WINTER FAMILY

Glistening like newly fallen snow, this jolly family is created from clay modeled over foam forms.

WHAT YOU'LL NEED

for snow boy

2- and 3-inch-diameter foam balls, such as Styrofoam
Craft stick
Five black-headed quilting pins
Red oven-bakeable clay, such as Sculpey
¾×12-inch piece of yellow-and-white gingham fabric
Red, fine-line permanent marking pen
Green acrylic paint
Felt scraps in royal blue, green, red, and yellow
Pinking shears
Round toothpick
Yellow paint
Yellow crafting foam

for snow dad

3-, 4-, and 5-inch-diameter foam balls, such as Styrofoam
Red oven-bakeable clay, such as Sculpey
Two black-headed map pins
Four black-headed quilting pins
White ankle sock
White sewing thread
Sewing needle
Fabric stiffener
Acrylic paints in tan, royal blue, red, and white
Paintbrush
½-inch red pom-pom
12-inch-long piece of ¼-inch-wide red-and-white polka-dot ribbon
Straight pins

for snow mom

3- and 5-inch-diameter foam balls, such as Styrofoam
Craft stick
Two black-headed map pins
Oven-bakeable clay, such as Sculpey, in red, green, pink, white, and yellow
4-inch straw doll hat
10-inch piece of ¼-inch-wide plaid ribbon
14-inch-long piece of ¼-inch-wide dark red grosgrain ribbon
12-inch-long piece of 1¼-inch-wide plaid fabric
Straight pins
Red acrylic paint

for snow baby

1- and 2-inch-diameter foam balls, such as Styrofoam
Five black-headed quilting pins
Orange oven-bakeable clay, such as Sculpey
Yellow infant sock
Yellow sewing thread
Sewing needle
¼-inch white pom-pom

for all snow family

Toothpicks
Thick white crafts glue
4 packages of white Crayola Model Magic Clay
Waxed paper
Rolling pin
Water
Crafts knife
Hot-glue gun and hot-glue sticks
Pink acrylic paint
Paintbrush
Black fine-line permanent marking pen
Scissors
Iridescent paint-on glitter

HERE'S HOW

1 *To make the Snow Boy*, cut off the top and bottom of the 3-inch foam ball. Cut the bottom off the 2-inch ball. Place two toothpicks in the 3-inch ball where the layers will join. Spread glue on the cut flat surfaces where the balls will meet.

2 With the 3-inch ball on the bottom, press the 2-inch ball onto the toothpicks for the head. Let the glue dry.

3 Cut a craft stick in half. Poke the flat ends of the sticks into each side of the Snow Boy, pointing upward. Glue in place. Let dry.

4 *To make the Snow Dad*, cut off the top and bottom of the 4- and 5-inch foam balls. Trim the bottom off the 3-inch ball. Place two toothpicks where each layer will join. Spread glue on the cut flat surfaces of the foam balls where the balls will meet. With the 5-inch ball on the bottom, press the 4-inch ball onto the toothpicks. Press the flat side of the 3-inch ball onto the center ball for the head. Let the glue dry.

continued on page 52

THE WINTER FAMILY *continued*

5 *To make the Snow Mom,* barely cut off the top and bottom of the 5-inch foam ball. Trim the bottom off the 3-inch ball. Place two toothpicks where the layers will join. Spread glue on the cut flat surfaces where the balls will meet. With the 5-inch ball on the bottom, press the flat side of the 3-inch ball onto the bottom ball for the head. Let the glue dry. Cut a craft stick in half. Poke the flat ends of the sticks into each side of the Snow Mom, pointing down. Glue in place. Let dry.

6 *For the Snow Baby,* cut off the top of the 1- and 2-inch foam balls. Place a toothpick where the layers will join. Spread glue on the cut flat surfaces of the foam balls, and press together. Let the glue dry.

7 *For all snow people,* tear off two pieces of waxed paper. Unwrap a package of white clay, and place between layers of waxed paper. Use a rolling pin to flatten the clay to about ¼-inch thick.

8 Place the sheet of clay over a foam snowman form. With wet fingers, mold the clay onto the shape. Shape the clay over the craft sticks to make arms for the boy and the mom. Shape clay arms for the baby and dad, using the photograph, *page 51,* as a guide. Cut away any excess clay using a crafts knife. Push the pin eyes and buttons into the wet clay. Arrange the snow people as desired, placing the dad's left arm around the baby, and his right arm on the mom's shoulder. If necessary, use toothpicks to hold the shapes together. Let the clay air dry as instructed by the manufacturer.

9 Form the red round, and orange carrot-shape noses out of oven-bakeable clay. Form small flowers and leaves for the mom's hat and a tiny leaf for her cherry nose. Bake in oven as directed by the manufacturer. Let cool. Press noses into clay to make an indentation. Glue into place using hot glue. Let dry.

10 Paint on glitter medium, covering snow people as well as possible. Let dry.

11 For the dad's and the baby's hats, place socks over heads. Mark size with a pin, remove, and handstitch to fit. Place hats on snowmen's heads. Pin in place if needed.

Paint hats with fabric stiffener, and let dry according to the manufacturer's instructions. Paint the dad's hat tan. Let dry. Add red and blue stripes on the top. Let dry. Glue a red pom-pom to the hat top. Let dry. For the baby's hat, paint thin red stripes around the hat. Let dry. Glue a white pom-pom on the tip of the hat. Let dry.

12 Tie the polka-dot ribbon around the dad's neck. Trim the ends.

13 For the mom's scarf, glue the red grosgrain ribbon to the edge of the plaid fabric. Let dry. Fray the outer fabric edge. Tie the scarf around the mom's neck. Trim ribbon ends. Glue the plaid ribbon around the straw hat. Glue the flowers over the ribbon intersection. Let dry. Pin the hat in place on the mom.

14 For the boy's scarf, use a red marking pen to add red lines to gingham fabric. Fray the ends, and color with red pen. Add green dots by dipping the handle end of a paintbrush into paint and dotting onto the surface. Let the paint dry. Wrap the scarf around the boy's neck.

15 For the boy's hat, cut four 1-inch-long narrow triangles from green and blue felt. Cut eight red triangles. Glue at an angle on boy's head as shown, *right.* Cut a ¼-inch-wide strip from yellow felt, cutting one side with straight scissors and the other with pinking shears. Glue around bottom edge of hat triangles, cutting end to fit. Break a toothpick in half. Paint it yellow. Let dry. Poke the sharp end of the toothpick into the center of the hat. Glue in place. Use a paper punch to cut a tiny circle from yellow foam. Cut two ¼-inch teardrop shapes from another piece of yellow foam. Glue the points of the teardrops to one side of the yellow circle, forming a propeller. Glue to the tip of the toothpick. Let dry.

16 For all snow people, paint round cheeks pink. Let dry. Using marking pen, draw in eyebrows, mouths, and cherry stem. Paint red lips on the mom. Let dry.

SMILING SNOWMAN

This grinning snow friend says "Merry Christmas" for all to see. Standing nearly four feet tall, he makes quite a front-yard attraction.

WHAT YOU'LL NEED

Tracing paper
Pencil
Ruler
40×46-inch piece of ¼-inch-thick masonite
Jigsaw
Sandpaper
Tack cloth
White spray primer
Paintbrushes
Acrylic paints in white, light blue, red, black, pink, blue, yellow, and green
Two 1-inch-diameter wood doll heads
3½-inch-diameter foam ball, such as Styrofoam
Knife
Decorative pom-pom trim for scarf
Strong adhesive, such as Liquid Nails
Screws
Screwdriver
3-foot-long wood stake for back

HERE'S HOW

1 Enlarge and trace the pattern, *page 57,* onto tracing paper. Transfer the pattern to masonite. Trace the button and flower patterns on *page 56.*

2 Cut out the snowman shape using a jigsaw. Sand the rough edges. Wipe away dust using a tack cloth.

3 In a well-ventilated work area, prime both the front and back sides of the snowman using white spray primer. Let the paint dry.

4 Paint the white areas first. Add a small amount of light blue paint to the paintbrush while the white paint is still wet. Add blue shading around his bottom, under his arms, next to the scarf, under the hat brim, eyes, nose, and peppermint buttons. Blend the blue shadow into the white as shown in the photograph, *opposite.* Using very little pink paint on a brush, paint the cheek areas.

5 Paint the scarf, hat brim, and hat ball yellow. Let dry. Paint the hat sections using multi colors as shown on the pattern. Let dry. Add a small amount of black to an almost dry brush. Softly brush on a dark shadow just above the yellow brim. If desired, add more black layers until you are satisfied with the color of the shadow.

6 Add details to the scarf and hat. To make the diagonal pattern of tiny dots, dip the handle end of a paintbrush into paint, and dot onto the surface. Make flowers the same way, except use a ½-inch-diameter dowel for the red and a round eraser end of a pencil for the white centers. Add leaves. Paint larger red dots onto ball on hat.

7 Paint the wood doll heads black. Let dry.

8 Cut a 3½-inch foam ball in half, and paint it red. Let dry. Add a white highlight.

9 Cut pieces of decorative pom-pom trim to accent the scarf. Glue at the ends of the scarf.

10 Transfer the peppermint button patterns onto the ¼-inch-thick wood. Cut out three buttons. Sand, and wipe off the dust with a tack cloth. Paint the buttons white. Let the paint dry. Add red stripes and a yellow center. Paint the leaves green.

11 Outline areas in black as indicated on the pattern. Let the paint dry.

12 Mark three spots on the snowman to indicate the button placement. Attach a wood stake to the back of snowman, and screw on at each button spot. Glue peppermint buttons over screws.

SMILING SNOWMAN *continued*

SMILING SNOWMAN
BUTTON PATTERN

SMILING SNOWMAN
FLOWER PATTERN

SMILING SNOWMAN PATTERN

1 SQUARE = 2 INCHES

ST. NICK STOCKINGS

Wonderful winter socks are transformed into one-of-a-kind holiday stockings, ready to be filled with the season's treasures.

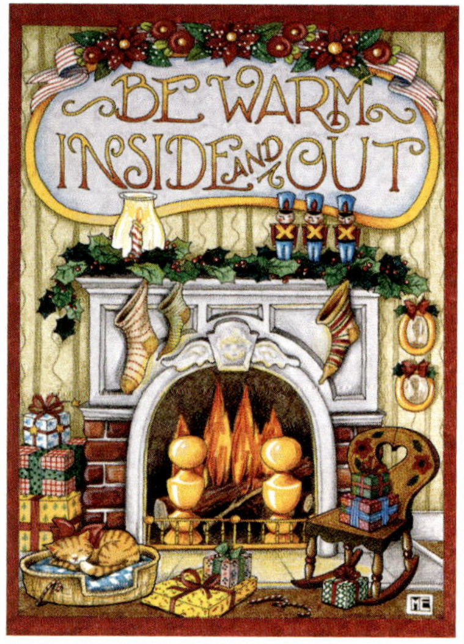

WHAT YOU'LL NEED
for the white stocking

Pencil; tracing paper
Purchased white sock
Fusible transweb paper
9×6-inch piece of gold imitation suede
Matching thread
Pinking shears, optional
3 packages of ½-inch-wide variegated Christmas red, 100% silk embroidery ribbon
5mm red beads
Red-and-white striped ribbon
Red jingle bell
1-inch plastic ring

for the silver stocking

Pencil; tracing paper
Purchased silver sock
Fusible transweb paper
9×6-inch piece of gold imitation suede
Matching thread
4×4-inch piece each of three different shades of green imitation suede for leaves
Green thread
5mm red beads
3 packages of ¼-inch-wide green, 100% silk embroidery ribbon
3 silver jingle bells
1-inch plastic ring

HERE'S HOW

1 *For both stockings*, draw an approximate 3×3-inch heel shape and a 4½×2½-inch toe shape, using sock as a pattern for the outer edges. Refer to the photograph, *opposite*, to draw the pattern for the inside edges. Trace the shapes, and a pair in reverse, onto transweb paper. Fuse to imitation suede following the manufacturer's instructions. Cut out.

2 Machine topstitch along inside curve, close to the edge. If desired, use pinking shears to pink the inside edge. With wrong sides facing in pairs, topstitch together close to the outer edge of both the heel and toe shapes.

3 Slip the heel and toe shapes onto the stocking, and fuse in place following the manufacturer's instructions.

4 *For trim on the white stocking*, add running stitches with silk ribbons in horizontal stripes around stocking. Add red beads to the spaces between the silk ribbon stitches. Trim top with a striped ribbon bow and jingle bell.

5 *For trim on the silver stocking*, trace the holly leaf pattern, *below*, onto tracing paper. Use the pattern to transfer five holly leaves onto transweb paper. Fuse to shades of green imitation suede, and cut out the leaves. Detail the leaf veins with machine satin stitches. Arrange the leaves using the photo, *opposite*, as a guide. Fuse to the stocking, adding hand stitches if necessary. Add red beads at the top of the holly leaves to resemble berries. Work rows of running stitches around the cuff using green silk ribbon.

6 *For the hanger*, use red pearl cotton to crochet around the ring if desired. Attach the ring to the corner of the stocking.

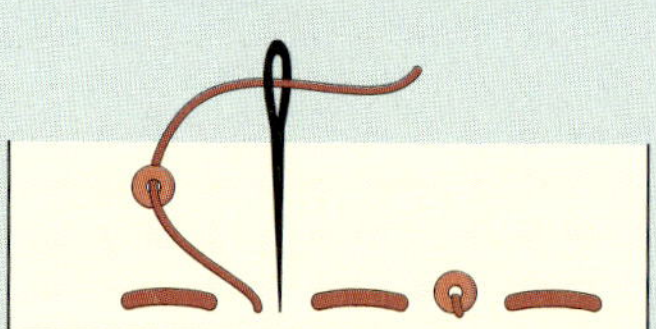
ADDING BEADS DIAGRAM

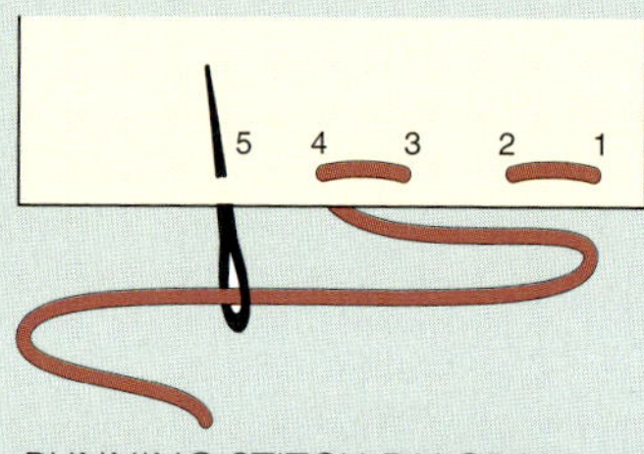

RUNNING STITCH DIAGRAM

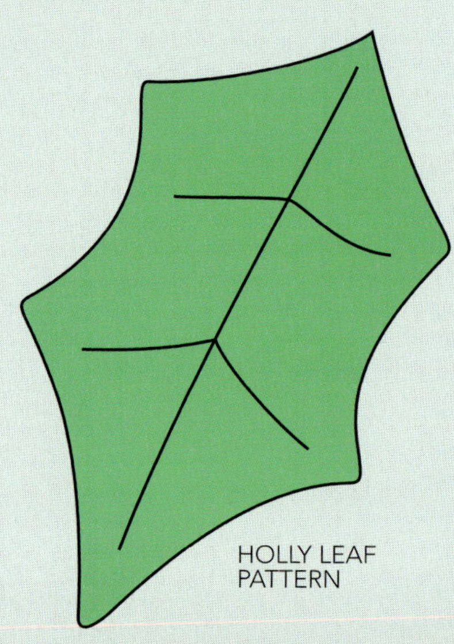
HOLLY LEAF PATTERN

POINSETTIA SWAG

Mary's holiday artwork is the inspiration for this everlasting decoration that will give a warm welcome at any threshold. Turn to page 62 for instructions.

BE WARM
INSIDE AND OUT

POINSETTIA SWAG *continued*

WHAT YOU'LL NEED

24-inch-long foam floral swag form, such as Styrofoam
¼ yard green felt to cover form and for leaves
Thick white crafts glue
Tracing paper
Pencil
10×12-inch piece of contrasting green felt for leaves
¼ yard each of two shades of red felt
Thread
Scraps of medium weight non-woven interfacing for base of poinsettias
Awl
24 pearl bridal sprays, each 8 inches long
Three 1⅛-inch gold jingle bells
Green embroidery floss; needle
Scrap of medium-weight cardboard
Poly-fil or batting for circle flowers
Six ¾-inch yellow buttons
3 yards of 1½-inch-wide red-and-white striped ribbon
3/4-inch-wide red with gold-edge wired ribbon

HERE'S HOW

1 Using the foam swag form as a guide, cut green felt to cover the swag shape, allowing for the thickness of the form. Glue felt over the foam shape, covering the front and back.

2 Trace the poinsettia and leaf patterns onto tracing paper. For each of the three poinsettias, cut five large petals and five medium petals from shades of red felt. Cut three to four leaves from green.

3 To assemble each poinsettia, make a boxed pleat at base of each petal, and hand stitch to secure. Hand-stitch five large petals to interfacing, rotating out from the center. Repeat with five medium petals spaced between first petals. Trim interfacing around stitching. Make three poinsettias. For each center, use an awl to poke a hole in the flower center. Slip and glue pearl spray into hole at back side. Add a jingle bell.

4 For leaves, make a pleat at the base as for petals. For veins, embroider stem stitches through the center with three plies of green floss, pulling stitches tightly to shape leaf. Make three to four leaves for each poinsettia.

5 For each circle flower, cut a 5-inch circle from red felt, and two leaves from green felt. Cut a 1½-inch circle from medium-weight cardboard.

6 Gather the outside edge of each felt circle around the cardboard piece, pulling tightly. Secure thread. Add poly-fil or batting to the center for padding. Gathered side will be the wrong side of flower. Use an awl to poke a hole into the flower center. Sew buttons to the center through the hole while using the 1½-inch circle of cardboard on the back side for support. Pull threads tightly to tuft center of flower. Make six flowers. To make slightly different size circles, vary the tension of gathered thread. For leaves, make a small boxed pleat at center, and hand stitch to secure.

7 To assemble the swag, glue striped ribbon across the entire length, making a 3-inch loop at each end with tails trimmed in a wedge, extending 2 inches beyond the loop.

8 Using the photograph on *pages 60–61* as a guide, glue the poinsettias on first. Fill in with leaves and circle flowers. To each side, add another ribbon loop with tail. Glue the center of the gold-edged red ribbon below the center poinsettia. Curl the ribbon ends.

POINSETTIA ASSEMBLY DIAGRAMS

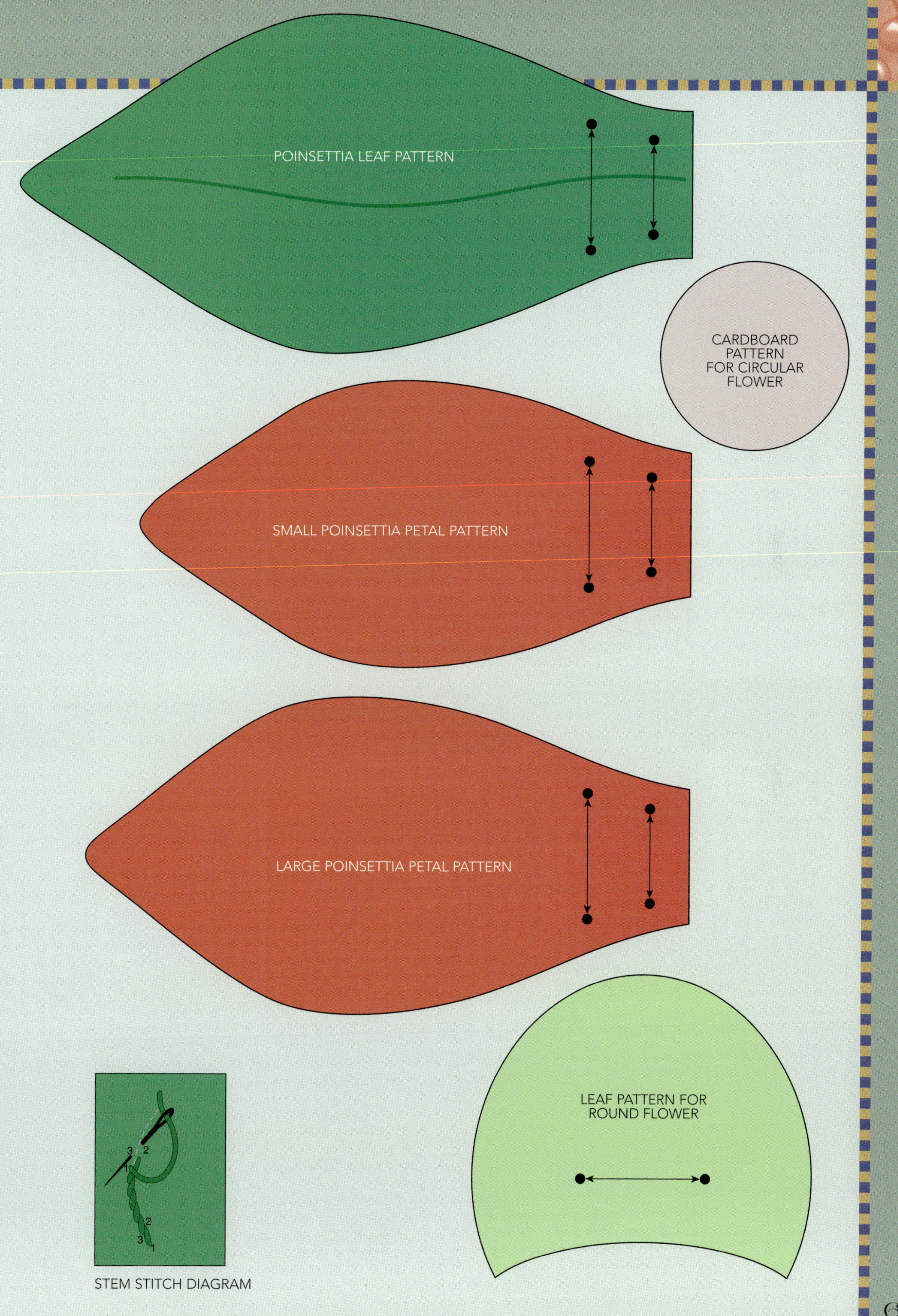
POINSETTIA LEAF PATTERN
CARDBOARD PATTERN FOR CIRCULAR FLOWER
SMALL POINSETTIA PETAL PATTERN
LARGE POINSETTIA PETAL PATTERN
LEAF PATTERN FOR ROUND FLOWER
STEM STITCH DIAGRAM

FLORAL KINDLING CARRIER

As pretty as it is practical, this bright red carrier makes stacking wood a cinch. It's trimmed with floral cross-stitched banding inspired by Mary's festive flowers.

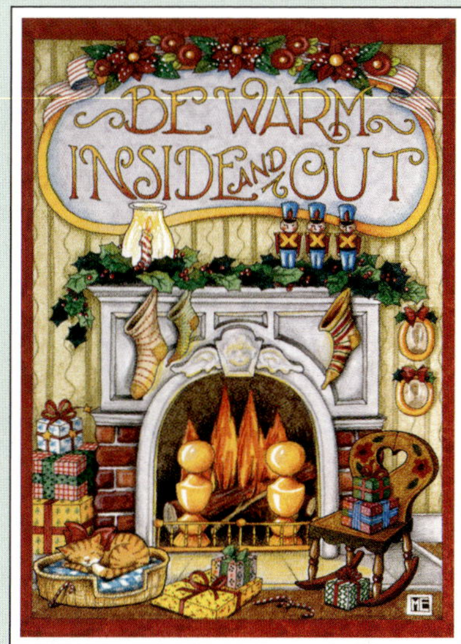

WHAT YOU'LL NEED

Two 24-inch-long pieces of 14-count red-edged, 3¼-inch-wide banding
Cotton embroidery floss as listed in key, page 66
Needle
Tracing paper; pencil
¾ yard red heavyweight fabric
¾ yard red lining fabric
Straight pins
4 yards of gold, double-fold bias tape
Two ¾-inch dowels, each 19½ inches long
Red acrylic paint
Paintbrush

HERE'S HOW

1 Find the center of one end of the banding. Measure down 3 inches. Begin stitching top center of chart, *page 67*, at that point. Use three plies of embroidery floss to work all cross-stitches over two threads of fabric. Repeat the pattern five times (or more for a bigger carrier) for each banding piece. Press finished stitchery from the back.

2 Enlarge and trace the carrier pattern/diagram, *page 66*. (For a larger carrier, lengthen as desired.) Cut shape from red heavyweight and lining fabrics. Pin fabrics wrong sides together. Position banding strips down each side and pin in place. Stitch the banding to the red fabrics along the banding edges.

3 Stitch bias tape along sides and U shapes. Fold the remaining raw edges under ¼ inch. To make casings, fold 2 inches of each carrier end to back side. Stitch along the edge to secure, without stitching through the banding.

4 Paint the dowels red. Let the paint dry. Insert the dowels into casings for handles.

FLORAL KINDLING CARRIER *continued*

Anchor	DMC
002	000 White
218	319 Pistachio
1025	347 Salmon
267	470 Avocado
326	720 Bittersweet
304	741 Tangerine
035	892 Carnation
255	907 Parrot green
862	934 Deep pine green
268	937 True pine green
382	3371 Black-brown
1015	3777 Terra-cotta
897	3857 Rosewood

BLENDED NEEDLE

239 702 Christmas green (1X) and
244 987 Forest green (1X)

BACKSTITCH

403 310 Black – poinsettia and leaves (1X)

382 3371 Black-brown – small flowers and leaves (1X)

Stitch count: *73 high x 31 wide*

Finished design sizes:
14-count fabric – 5¼ x 2¼ inches
16-count fabric – 4½ x 2 inches
18-count fabric – 4 x 1¾ inches

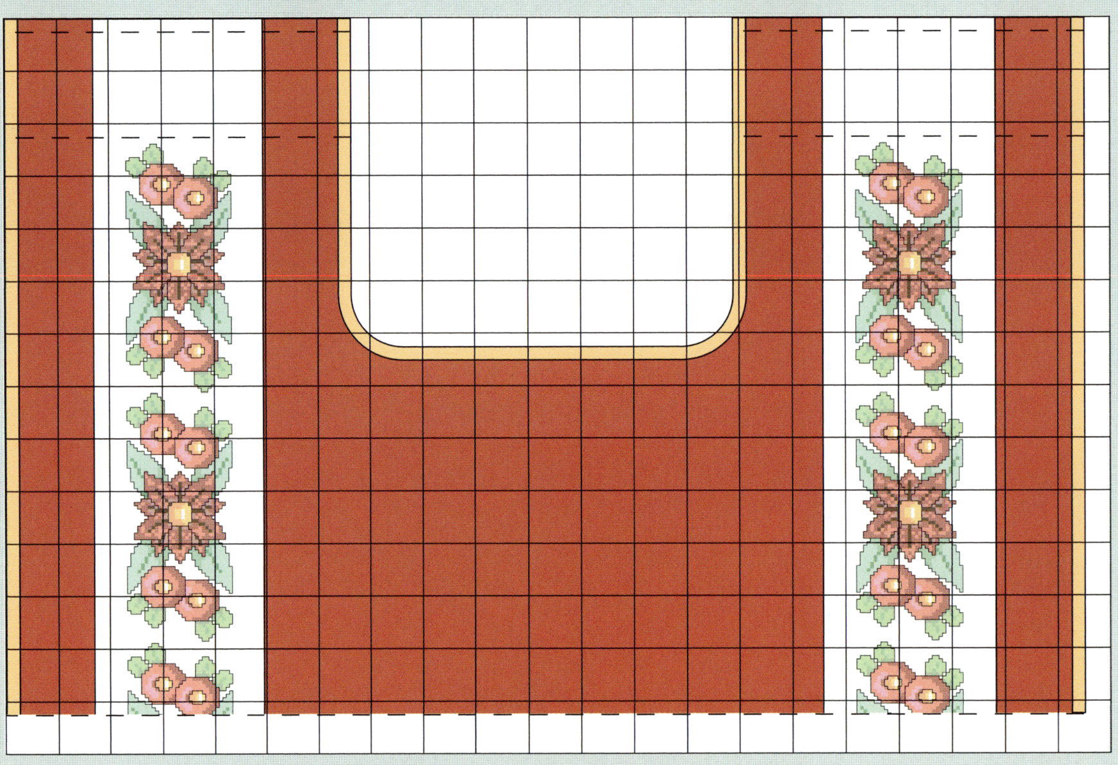

FLORAL KINDLING CARRIER PATTERN/DIAGRAM 1 SQUARE = 1 INCH

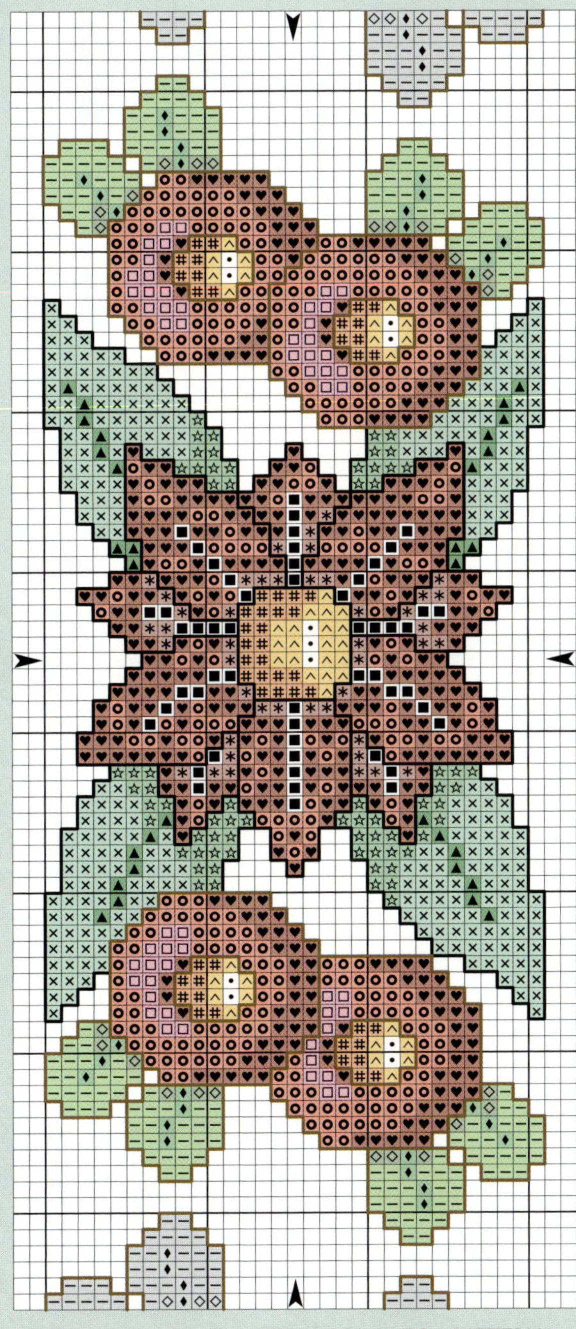

FLORAL KINDLING CARRIER CROSS-STITCH PATTERN
(Gray areas indicate where pattern repeats.)

FESTIVE TABLE MAT

Cheery checks border this delightful appliquéd table mat in vibrant seasonal colors, resembling the saddle on Mary's reindeer.

WHAT YOU'LL NEED

⅝ yard of white lining fabric
Tracing paper
Pencil
Fabric marking pencil
½ yard of red print fabric for center background
½ yard of green print fabric for background
⅝ yard of yellow fabric for appliqué border
Fusible transweb paper
Rayon machine-embroidery thread in red, yellow, and green
¼ yard of green fabric for mitered sashing
1 yard of red cotton fabric for patchwork and back
⅓ yard of white fabric for patchwork and binding
12 white ½-inch sew-through pearl buttons
8 gold tassels, each 2 inches long with a ½-inch loop
Four ½-inch large-hole green wood beads
4 gold 1½-inch cutout star charms

HERE'S HOW

1 Cut a 20×20-inch piece of white lining fabric. Enlarge and trace the red-and-white checked center portion of the table mat from *page 71*. Turn and repeat. Repeat two more times to make a full-size pattern for the center. Use a fabric pencil to trace the full-size center pattern, and center on the lining fabric. This will include the red and green print backgrounds, yellow border, red triangles, and 1×1-inch red appliqué squares.

2 Trace each of these individual pieces onto fusible transweb paper, and fuse to the corresponding fabric following the manufacturer's instructions. Cut out the pieces, allowing ⅛ inch extra where applicable to slip under adjacent appliqué pieces and ¼ inch for seam at outer edge.

3 Using the traced pattern on the lining as a guide, fuse all appliqué pieces to the lining. Machine-satin-stitch or close zigzag with matching threads. Trim lining fabric while squaring center, allowing a ¼-inch seam.

4 Cut four green sashing strips, each 1¼×20 inches. Center and stitch sashing along appliqué, mitering at corners and trimming excess sashing.

5 Cut 80 red and 80 white fabric squares, each 1½×1½ inches. Piece 18 squares in checkerboard fashion for two rows, and stitch to green sashing as shown on the diagram, *page 70*. Repeat for remaining sides, making two rows of 22.

6 Layer runner top with red backing fabric. Trim even. Baste around outside edge. Bind outside edge with white fabric, making a ⅜-inch binding.

7 Use red thread to sew a white button to the center of each red appliquéd square in the center of the mat.

8 Slip two tassel loops through a green bead, and stitch to one corner of the mat, then add a star charm. Repeat for the remaining corners.

FESTIVE TABLE MAT *continued*

FESTIVE TABLE MAT DIAGRAM

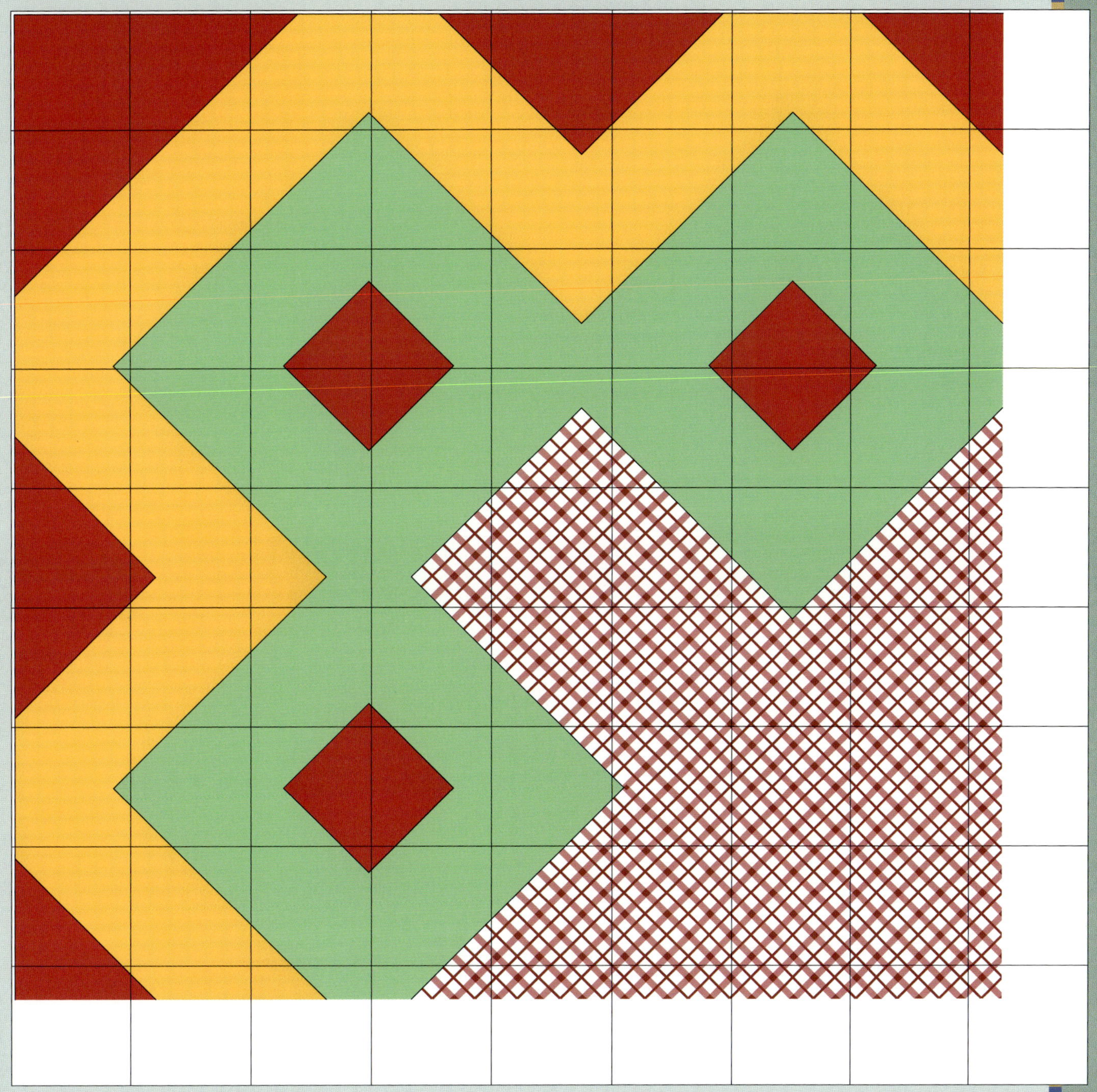

FESTIVE TABLE MAT QUARTER PATTERN

1 SQUARE = 1 INCH

DASHING REINDEER PILLOW

Laden with details and loving stitches, this proud member of Santa's herd is a grand accent to any room. The key is below. *The chart is on pages 74–77.*

WHAT YOU'LL NEED

- 14x20-inch piece of 28-count light blue Jobelan fabric
- Cotton embroidery floss as listed in key
- Needle
- Embroidery hoop
- ½ yard red wool fabric
- 17×24-inch piece of fleece
- Fusible interfacing, optional
- 2½ yards of red satin sew-in piping
- Surface attachments as listed in key
- 12×18-inch pillow form

HERE'S HOW

1 Tape or zigzag the edges of the Jobelan fabric to prevent fraying. Find the center of the chart and the center of the fabric. Begin stitching there.

Anchor	DMC
002	000 White
897	221 Shell pink
403	310 Black
9046	321 Christmas red
9575	353 Peach
235	414 Steel
374	420 Hazel
267	470 Avocado
212	561 Dark seafoam
210	562 Medium seafoam
590	712 Cream
305	725 Topaz
144	800 Delft blue
168	807 Peacock blue
1005	816 Garnet
882	945 Ivory
382	3371 Black-brown
1023	3712 Salmon
236	3799 Charcoal
313	3854 Autumn gold
BLENDED NEEDLE	
1049	301 Mahogany (2X) and
370	434 Medium chestnut (1X)
371	433 Dark chestnut (2X) and
382	3371 Black-brown (1X)
1068	924 Gray-blue (2X) and
236	3799 Charcoal (1X)
355	975 Golden brown (2X) and
371	433 Dark chestnut (1X)
355	975 Golden brown (2X) and
370	434 Medium chestnut (1X)
887	3045 Yellow-beige (2X) and
854	371 Pecan (1X)
397	3072 Beaver gray (2X) and
231	453 Shell gray (1X)
269	3362 Loden (2X) and
268	937 Pine green (1X)
382	3371 Black-brown (2X) and
371	433 Dark chestnut (1X)
1066	3809 Turquoise (2X) and
236	3799 Charcoal (1X)
BACKSTITCH	
403	310 Black – all other stitches (2X)
9046	321 Christmas red – collar (2X)
683	500 Blue-green – leaf veins (2X)
246	986 Forest green – stem (2X)
STRAIGHT STITCH	
9046	321 Christmas red – candy cane (2X)
305	725 Topaz – reins (6X)
246	986 Forest green – leaves at bottom (6X)
COUCHING	
9046	321 Christmas red – blanket (2X)
168	807 Peacock blue couched with
683	924 Gray-blue (3X) – twisted floss

SURFACE ATTACHMENTS

- Red 3mm pearl beads – snow
- Gold beads – beads between stars
- Green 6mm pearl beads – bottom of blanket
- Gold 8mm beads – hanging from rings
- Gold 10mm rings – on red ribbon
- Gold 16mm ring – middle ring
- Red 1/4-inch ribbon – reins
- Green 1/4-inch ribbon – antler
- 3/8-inch gold jingle bells – blanket
- White 5mm pom-poms – background
- Star charms – blanket and collar
- Star sequins with gold beads – reins

***Stitch count:** 137 high x 210 wide*

Finished design sizes:
28-count fabric – 9¾ x 15 inches
32-count fabric – 8½ x 13⅛ inches
36-count fabric – 7⅝ x 11⅝ inches

Use two plies of embroidery floss to work all cross-stitches over two threads of fabric.

2 Use the diagrams, *page 190*, to work the specialty stitches. Use the number of plies for each stitch as noted in the key. Press the finished stitchery from the back.

3 To finish, use ¼-inch seams with right sides facing unless otherwise indicated. From wool, cut two 2¼×20-inch horizontal and two 2¼×15-inch vertical miter strips.

4 Fuse interfacing to the wrong side of the wool fabric. Center and stitch miter strips horizontally and vertically at the edges of the design, mitering at the corners. Trim excess. Trim the cross-stitch fabric to include a ¼-inch seam. Carefully press. Cut the backing fabric the same size as the front. Stitch piping around the outside edge on the front. Stitch the front to the back leaving an opening for turning. Turn. Insert the pillow form. Stitch the opening closed. Add surface attachments as indicated in key.

REINDEER PILLOW *continued*

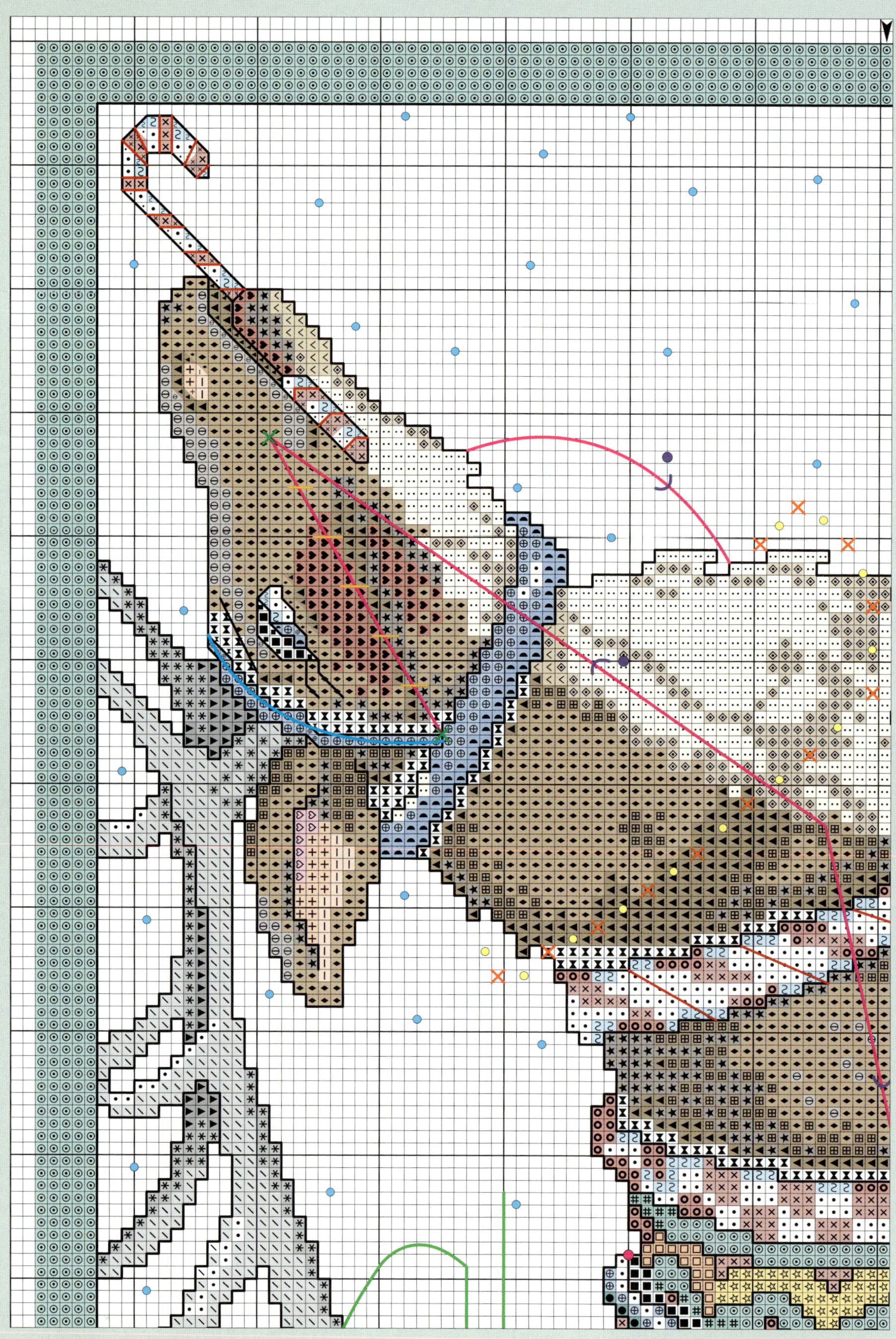

REINDEER PILLOW *continued*

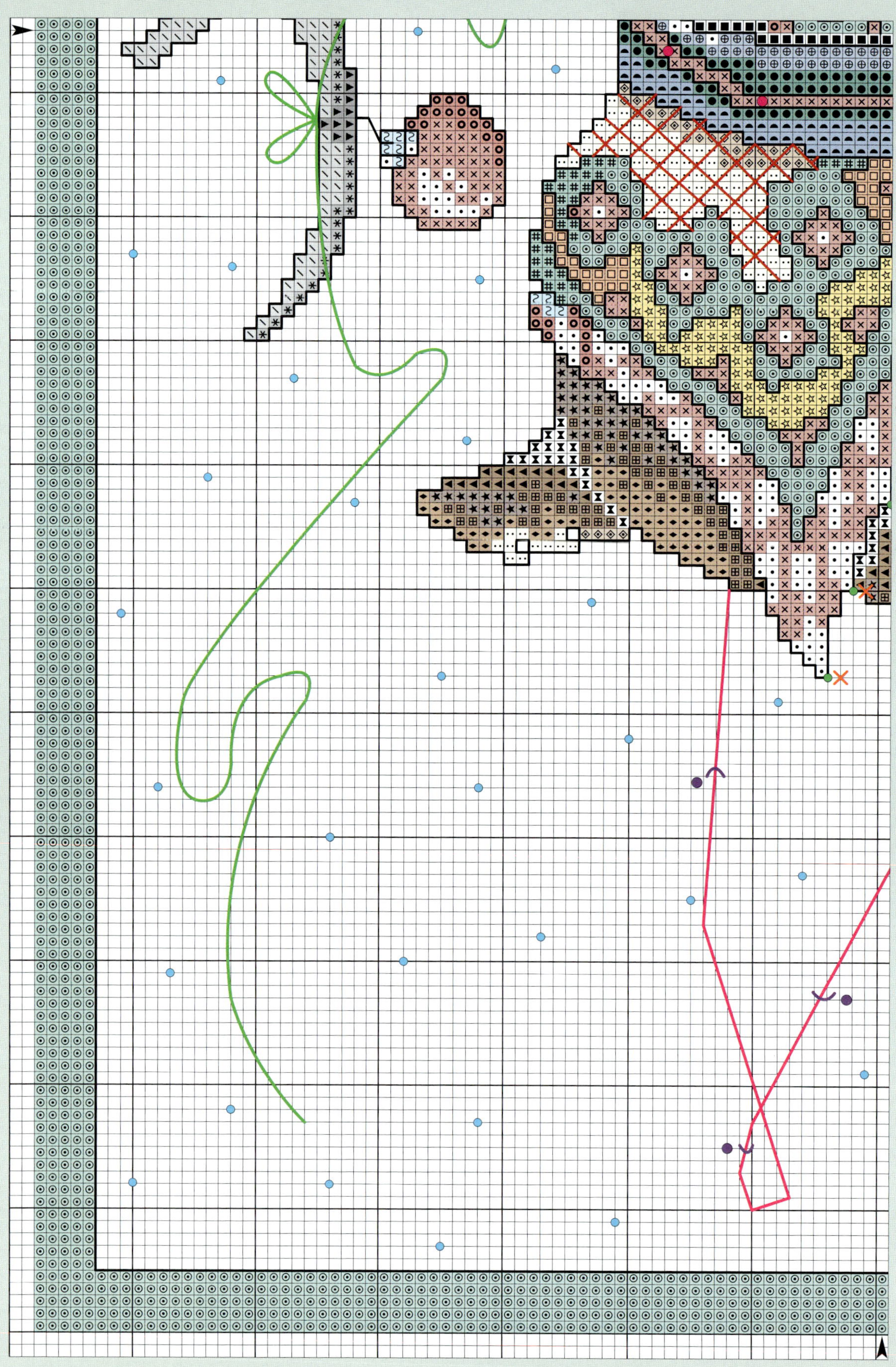

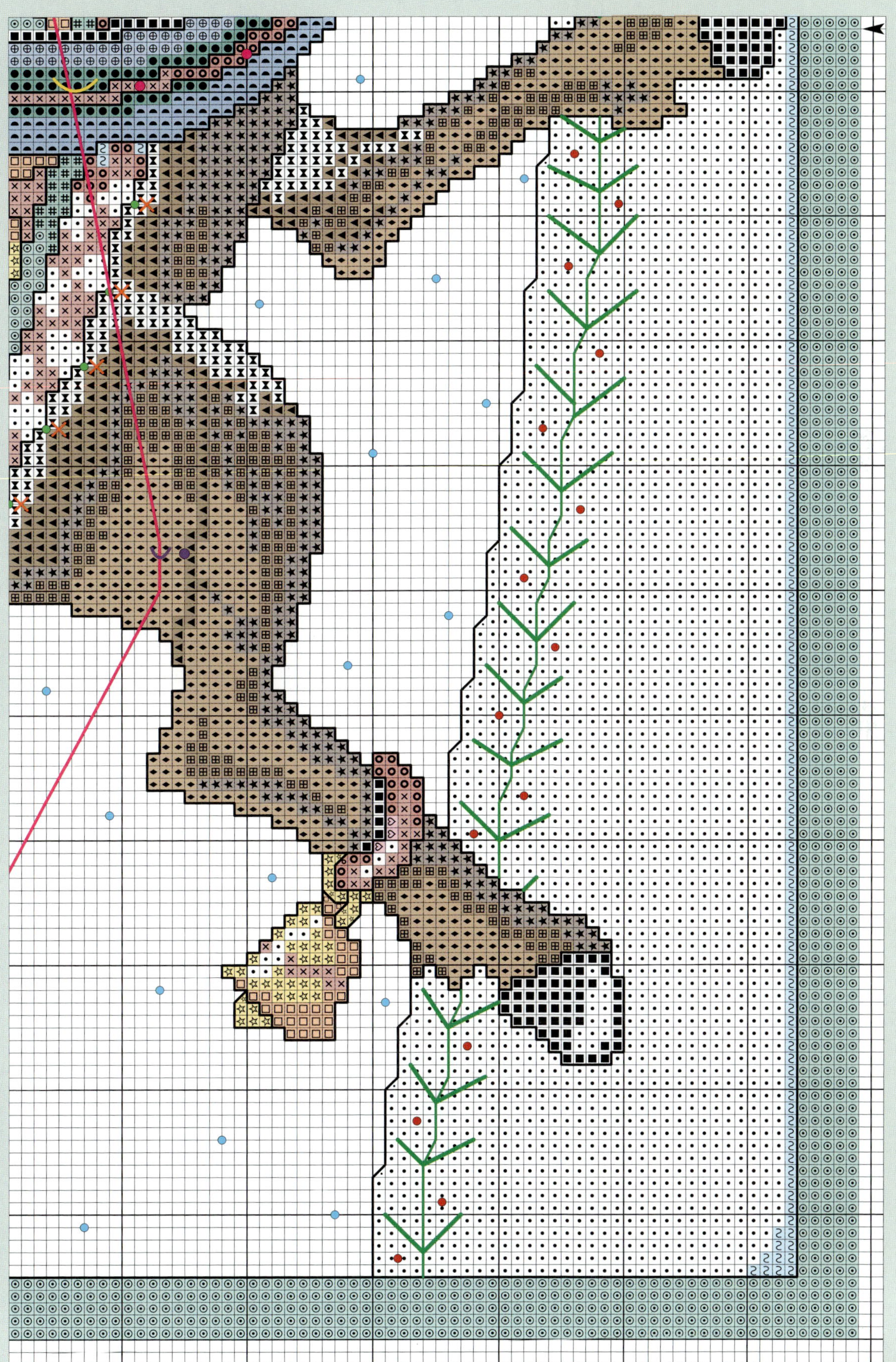

HOLIDAY CHEER FRAME

Bright buttons, beads, and colorful stitches dance on this whimsical felt frame, a fitting tribute to your favorite ol' elf.

WHAT YOU'LL NEED

Ruler; black marking pen
Two 8½×8½-inch red felt squares
Scissors; tracing paper; pencil
Felt scraps in red, yellow, and lime green
Straight pins; needle
Cotton embroidery floss in black, red, green, and bright orange
Approximately 25 yellow ½-inch buttons
Large red seed beads
Tape
Photo, greeting card, or other desired artwork
Thick white crafts glue
8¼×8¼-inch piece of medium-weight cardboard; easel

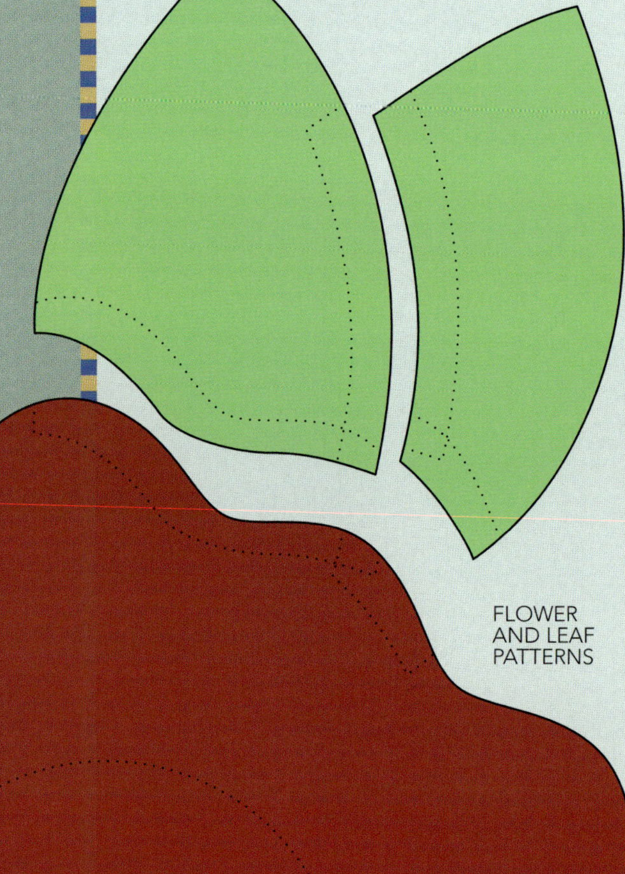

FLOWER AND LEAF PATTERNS

HERE'S HOW

1 Measure and mark a 3-inch square in the center of each of the red felt squares. Cut out the center squares.

2 Trace the flower and leaf patterns, *below left*. Use the patterns to cut the pieces from corresponding colors of felt.

3 Layer the felt squares, aligning the edges. Pin together. Arrange the flower and leaf felt pieces in one corner as shown in the photograph, *opposite*. Pin in place.

4 Use one strand of black embroidery floss to work blanket stitches, *page 190*, around the outside and inside edges of the square, and around the flower and leaf pieces. Remove pins.

5 Use one strand of green embroidery floss to work

French knots, *page 190,* as well as couched circles and lines on the leaves. Use orange embroidery floss for the couched flower center.

6 Sew on the buttons and beads using red embroidery floss. From the back, push the needle to the front side, going through a hole in the button. Slip on a seed bead, and push the needle through the remaining hole in the button. Continue adding buttons and beads in this manner, using the photo, *above,* as a placement guide.

7 Tape the desired picture in the center of the frame back. Carefully glue the cardboard piece on the back. Let dry. Place the frame in an easel to display.

JOLLY ST. NICK STOCKING

Based on Mary's famous SC greeting card, this splendid stitched and beaded stocking is destined to be treasured for many Christmases to come.

WHAT YOU'LL NEED

8x12-inch piece of 25-count red Lugana fabric
14x20-inch piece of 25-count black Lugana fabric
Cotton embroidery floss as listed in the key, page 82
Needle
Tracing paper
Pencil
White sewing pencil
Scissors
Surface attachments as listed in key
½ yard each of black wool fabric for back, red cotton for lining, fleece, and fusible interfacing
1½ yards of red sew-in piping
¾ yard of black piping
#5 red pearl cotton
Crochet hook
1-inch plastic ring
1 yard of 1½-inch-wide red satin ribbon

HERE'S HOW

1 Tape or zigzag the edges of the Lugana fabrics to prevent fraying. Find the center of the cuff chart, *pages 82–83,* and the center of the red Lugana fabric; begin stitching there. Use two plies of floss to work the cross-stitches over two threads of fabric. Work the specialty stitches, *pages 190–191,* as indicated in the key. Repeat for the stocking body on black.

2 Enlarge, trace, and cut out the pattern, *right.* Trace around shape on stitched stocking body, aligning pattern with stitchery. Trace around the pattern using a white sewing pencil.

3 Press finished pieces from the back. Attach beads using one ply of matching floss.

4 On stocking body, line the cross-stitched shape with fleece. Baste together. Cut out stocking, allowing ½ inch for seam. Cut out stocking back in the same manner.

5 Press fusible interfacing to wrong side of back. Stitch red piping on basting line. With right sides facing, stitch stocking front to back. Clip and trim seam. Turn to right side.

6 Cut a front and back lining piece from pattern, including a ½-inch seam. With right sides facing, stitch pieces together leaving an opening at the bottom edge for turning.

7 For cuff, cut cross-stitch fabric with the design centered on 7½x17-inch fabric rectangle. Line cuff with fleece. Sew short ends together.

8 Fold cuff in half, matching raw edges. Stitch seam. Add black piping around bottom edge of cuff. Baste cuff to top of stocking. With right sides facing, slip stocking into lining. Stitch around the top edge. Trim and clip seam. Pull stocking through opening in lining. Stitch opening in lining closed. Press lining to inside of the stocking.

9 Use red pearl cotton to single crochet around plastic ring. Stitch ring to stocking at back seam. Add a ribbon bow.

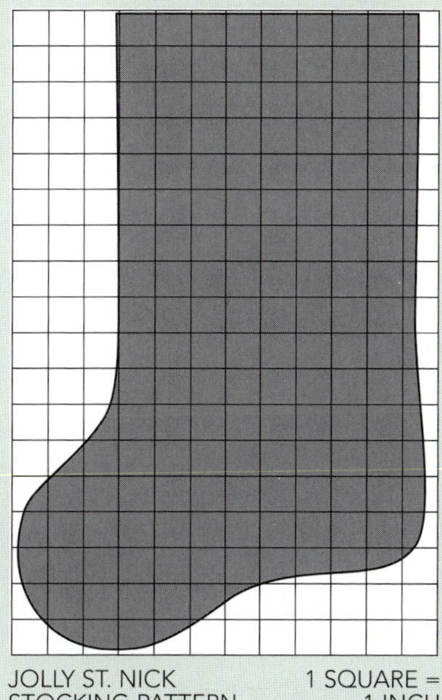

JOLLY ST. NICK STOCKING PATTERN — 1 SQUARE = 1 INCH

Anchor		DMC
002		000 White
897		221 Deep shell pink
1026		225 Pale shell pink
403		310 Black
9046		321 Christmas red
398		415 Pearl gray
1038		519 Sky blue
1062		597 Turquoise
074		604 Light cranberry
227		701 True Christmas green
361		738 Tan
304		741 Tangerine
144		800 Delft blue
047		817 Coral
332		946 Burnt orange
039		961 Dark rose-pink
297		973 Canary
268		3346 Hunter green
382		3371 Black-brown
025		3716 Light rose-pink
313		3825 Bittersweet
BLENDED NEEDLE		
9046 047		321 Christmas red (1X) and 817 Coral (1X)
257 256		703 True chartreuse (1X) and 906 Medium parrot green (1X)
132 164		797 Royal blue (1X) and 3842 Deep Wedgwood blue (1X)
255 265		907 Light parrot green (1X) and 704 Light chartreuse (1X)
341 1014		918 Red-copper (1X) and 355 Terra-cotta (1X)
054 063		956 Geranium (1X) and 602 Medium cranberry (1X)
075 039		962 Medium rose-pink (1X) and 961 Dark rose-pink (1X)
433 1039		996 Electric blue (1X) and 518 Light Wedgwood blue (1X)
360 1014		3031 Mocha (1X) and 355 Terra-cotta (1X)
HALF CROSS-STITCH (stitch in direction of symbol)		
398		415 Pearl gray – star glow (2X)
BACKSTITCH		
403		310 Black – all other stitches (2X)
9046		321 Christmas red – candy, dots on coat (2X)
228		700 Medium Christmas green – leaf detail (2X)
047		817 Coral – flower centers (2X)
045		902 Garnet – flowers on bottom of coat (2X)
STRAIGHT STITCH		
403		310 Black – flowers and leaves on cuff and coat (2X)
RUNNING STITCH		
045		902 Garnet – flowers on cuff and coat (2X)
LAZY DAISY		
403		310 Black – leaves at bottom of coat (2X)
257		703 True chartreuse – cuff, heel, and toe (2X)
FRENCH KNOT		
403		310 Black – flower centers, detail on coat
228		700 Medium Christmas green – leaf detail (3X wrapped once)
SURFACE ATTACHMENTS		
		Red beads – head
		Ruby ring bead with black seed bead – cuff, heel, and toe
		Black seed beads – cuff, heel, and toe
		Crystal seed beads – star

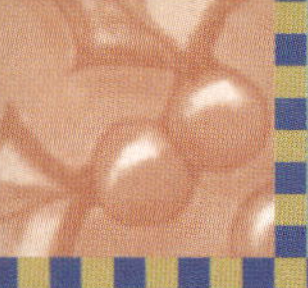

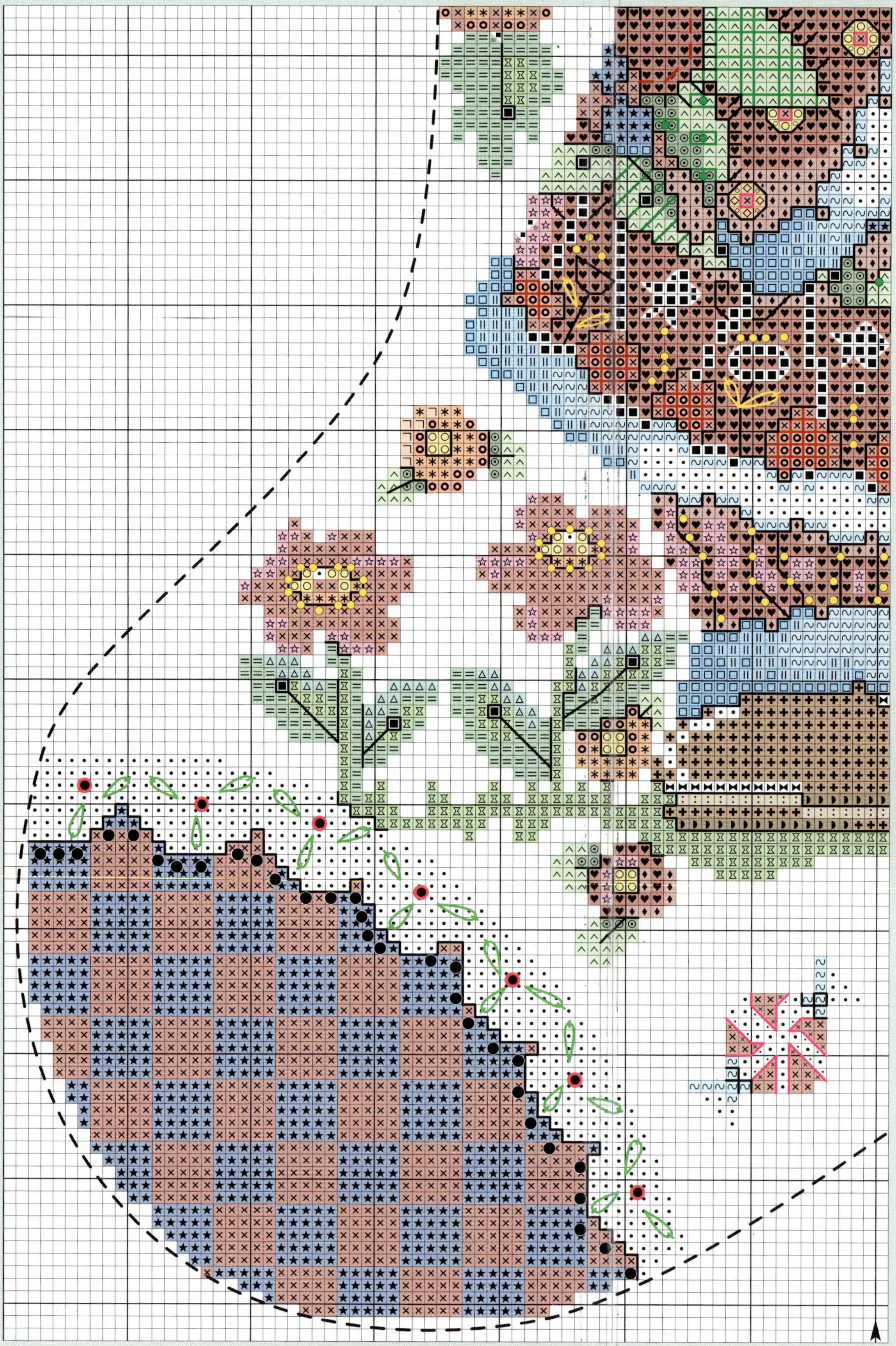

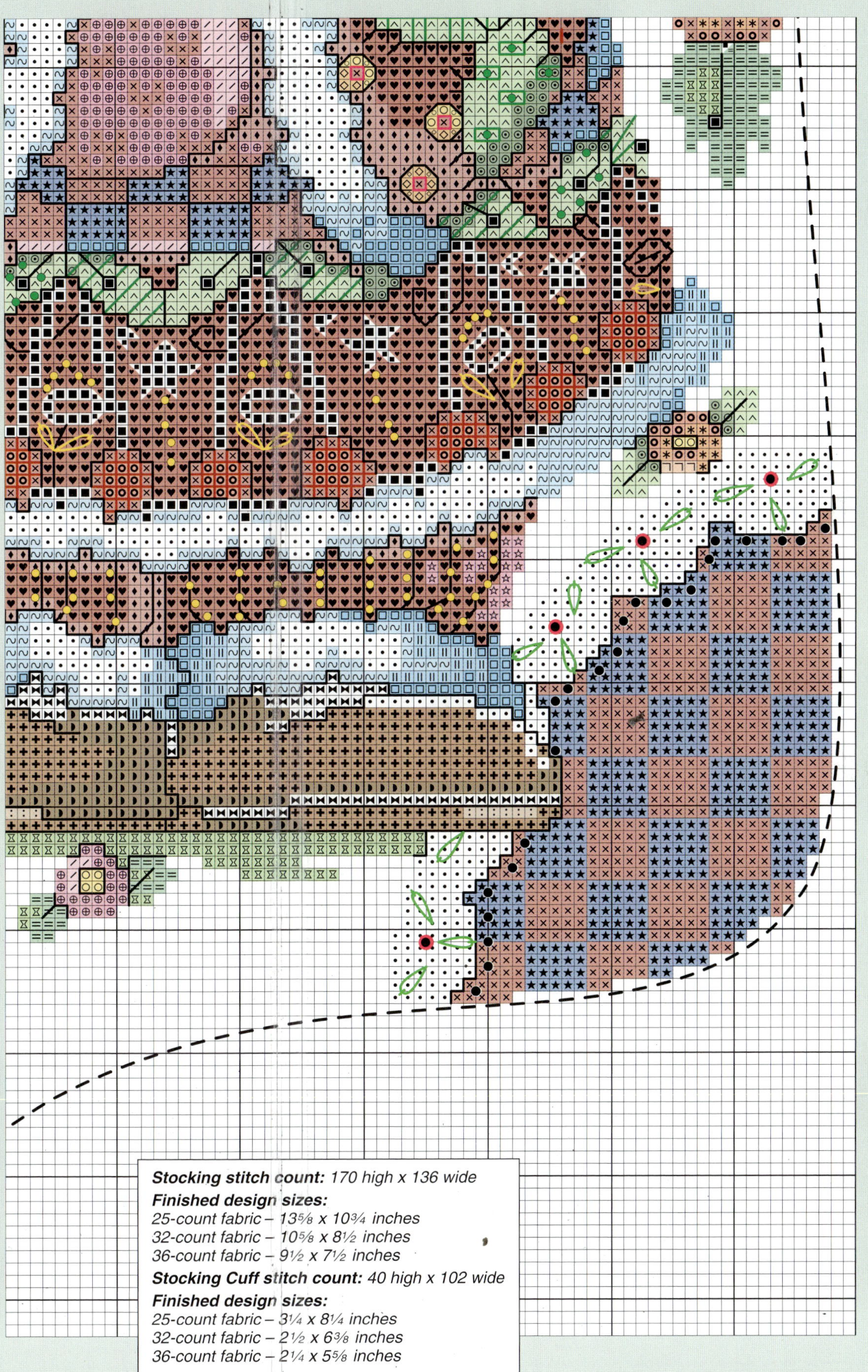

Stocking stitch count: 170 high x 136 wide

Finished design sizes:
25-count fabric – 13⅝ x 10¾ inches
32-count fabric – 10⅝ x 8½ inches
36-count fabric – 9½ x 7½ inches

Stocking Cuff stitch count: 40 high x 102 wide

Finished design sizes:
25-count fabric – 3¼ x 8¼ inches
32-count fabric – 2½ x 6⅜ inches
36-count fabric – 2¼ x 5⅝ inches

GIFTS FROM THE HEART

Put your talents to work during the giving season. No matter what your crafting talents are, you'll find a new favorite project derived from Mary's fanciful illustrations. In this chapter you'll find patchwork mittens, wood checkerboard sets, paper gift tags, fleece snowmen, and more—all handmade treasures you can make for the loved ones on your gift list.

MERRY MITTENS

These delightful mittens will keep hands warm even on the most blustery days.

WHAT YOU'LL NEED

Tracing paper
Pencil
Scissors
12×18-inch piece each of batting and cotton underlining fabric
⅛ yard each of eight different red and green calico fabrics
Fusible transweb paper
⅛ yard white calico for hearts
Black cotton embroidery floss
⅓ yard of red wool fabric for mitten palm and thumb
⅓ yard of white fleece for lining
¾ yard of ¼-inch-wide elastic
18 red 5mm faceted beads

HERE'S HOW

1 Enlarge and trace the patterns, *below right*, onto tracing paper. Cut out. Cut the batting and cotton underlining into two 12×9-inch pieces.

2 Using the calico fabrics, work two crazy patchwork pieces, large enough for mitten backs. Baste the pieces, centered, onto underlining fabrics.

3 Trace six heart shapes onto fusible transweb paper. Fuse to white calico. Cut out and fuse three hearts onto each hand back. Refer to the photograph, *opposite*, for placement.

4 Baste batting to wrong side of mitten backs. With two plies of black floss, add blanket-stitch details (*page 190*) to the edges of some of the patchwork and around each heart.

5 Use the patterns to cut two sets of mitten pieces from patchwork, wool, and fleece lining, reversing palm for the opposite mitten. Set lining aside.

6 Stitch all seams with right sides facing. Use a ¼-inch seam allowance.

7 Stitch the thumb to the thumb gusset around the curved edge from A to B. Stitch the inner seam of the thumb and palm, tapering to a point at A. Machine-zigzag over elastic stretched on the wrong side of the palm/thumb, 3 inches down from the top edge.

8 Stitch mitten palm to back along side and finger curve. Turn right side out. Repeat for lining, leaving an opening for turning in the side seam of the lining.

9 Slip the mitten into the lining, matching the side seams and the thumb. Stitch around the top edge.

10 Slip-stitch the opening in the lining closed. Tuck the lining into the mitten. Sew three beads in the center of each heart shape.

HEART PATTERN

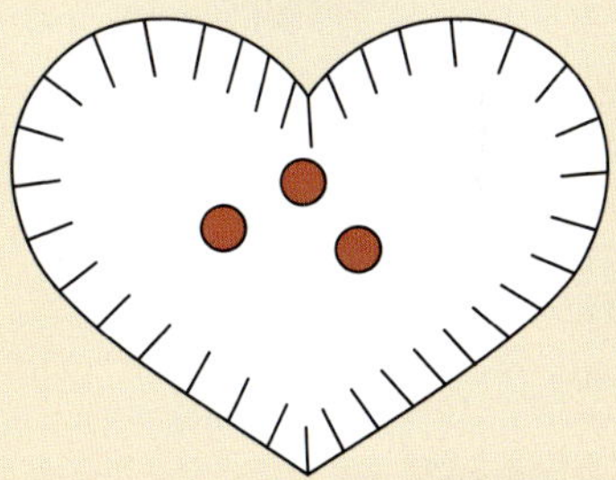

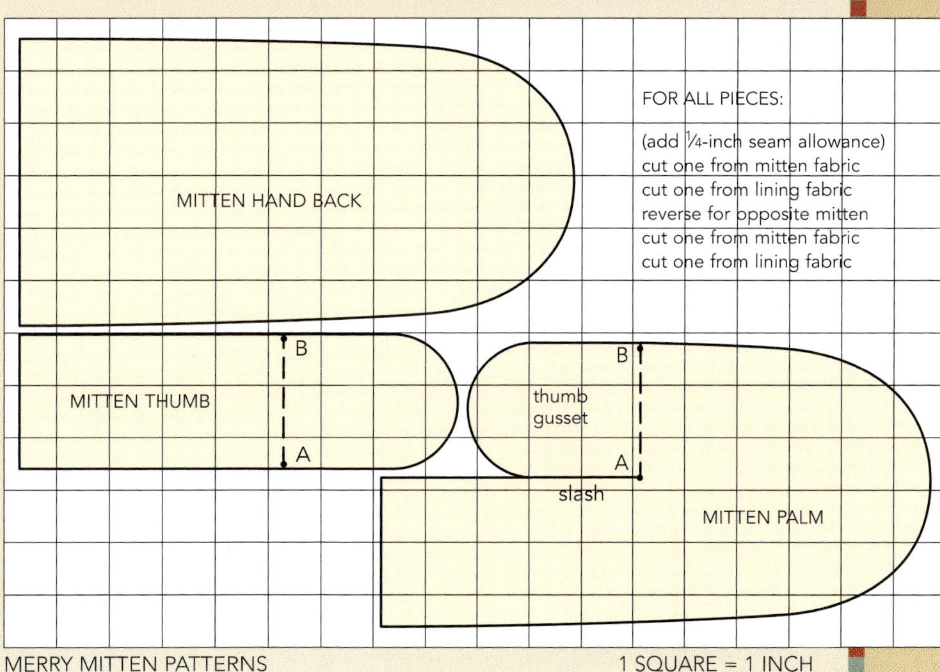

MERRY MITTEN PATTERNS 1 SQUARE = 1 INCH

HAPPY KNIT HAT

Little girls will stay toasty warm in this knit hat trimmed with a lazy daisy and duplicate stitch border. A pom-pom tops off this wooly winter wear.

WHAT YOU'LL NEED

Patons Classic Wool, (223 yards/3½ oz. per skein): one skein each of Old Gold (204), Winter White (201), Forest Green (241), Leaf Green (240), and Rich Red (207)

Size 7 straight knitting needles or size to obtain gauge, *right*

One size 7, 16-inch-length circular needle

One set of size 7 double-pointed knitting needles (dpn)

One ring-type stitch marker

Tapestry needle

HERE'S HOW

Gauge: In stockinette stitch (st st) and color patterns, 20 sts and 26 rows = 4 inches.

Notes: *When knitting with two colors in one row, carry the strand not in use loosely along the WS of the fabric. To change color, bring the next strand from under the present strand for a "twist" to prevent holes. Work parts of the flower panel with embroidery stitches after you complete the knitting. The bobbles at the center of each flower are best worked with separate strands.*

for hat

Beginning at the lower edge with forest green and the straight needles, CO 102 sts. P 1 row. K 1 row. P 1 row. Cut green and leave a tail to weave in later.

striped border

Row 1: * K 1 red, k 1 gold; rep from * across.

Row 2: * P 1 gold, k 1 red; rep from * across.

Rep rows 1–2 twice more; then rep Row 1 again. Cut gold and red, and leave long tails to weave in later.

green & white border

Row 1: With forest green, p across.

Row 2: * K 3 white, k 3 using leaf green; rep from * across.

Row 3: With forest green, p across.

flower border

Change to white and k across. P 1 row. K across next row increasing 66 sts evenly spaced * 168 sts. P 1 row, k 1 row, p 1 row.

Bobble Row: With white, k 6; * make a bobble with gold in the next st [(k 1, yo) twice, k 1; turn; k 5; turn; p 5; yb, slip second then third, fourth, and fifth sts over the first st * bobble made] **, k 13 with white; rep from * across ending last rep at **, k 7 with white. With white, beg with a p row, work 5 st st rows.

second green & white border

Row 1: With forest green, k across.

Row 2: * P 3 white, p 3 leaf green; rep from * across.

Row 3: With forest green, k across.

(continued on page 92)

HAPPY KNIT HAT *continued*

crown

Note: The crown is worked in rnds beginning with a circular needle, then changing to the dpn when necessary.

With the circular needle and gold, p across and turn so the RS is facing. Place a marker to indicate the beginning of the rnd; join. K 3 rnds.

Rnd 4: K around and dec 8 sts evenly spaced = 160 sts.

Rnds 5–7: Knit.

Rnd 8: (K 14, k2tog) around = 150 sts.

Rnds 9–11: Knit.

Rnd 12: (K 13, k2tog) around = 140 sts.

Rnds 13–15: Knit.

Rnd 16: (K 12, k2tog) around = 130 sts.

Rnds 17–19: Knit.

Rnd 20: (K 11, k2tog) around = 120 sts.

Rnds 21–23: Knit.

Rnd 24: (K 10, k 2 tog) around = 110 sts.

Rnd 25 and each following odd numbered rnd: Knit.

Rnd 26: (K 9, k2tog) around = 100 sts.

Rnd 28: (K 8, k2tog) around = 90 sts.

Rnd 30: (K 7, k2tog) around = 80 sts.

Rnd 32: (K 6, k2tog) around = 70 sts.

Rnd 34: (K 5, k2tog) around = 60 sts.

Rnd 36: (K 4, k2tog) around = 50 sts.

Rnd 38: (K2tog) around = 25 sts.

Leaving a long tail, cut yarn. Thread the tail into the tapestry needle and back through the rem 25 sts. Pull up to close opening, and secure in place.

finishing

For the embroidery, use a single strand of leaf green to duplicate-stitch the waves between the flowers; beg the chart at A and working to C; then rep B–C across ending last rep at D. With a double strand of the red, work lazy daisies as shown on the chart. Join side seam. Fold forest green border at lower edge in half, and whip st to inside of hat.

pom-pom

Wind gold yarn loosely around your hand about 50 times. Cut the yarn. Tie a separate strand of yarn around the center tightly, leaving long tails. Cut the loops at each end, and trim. With the tying strand, secure to top of the hat.

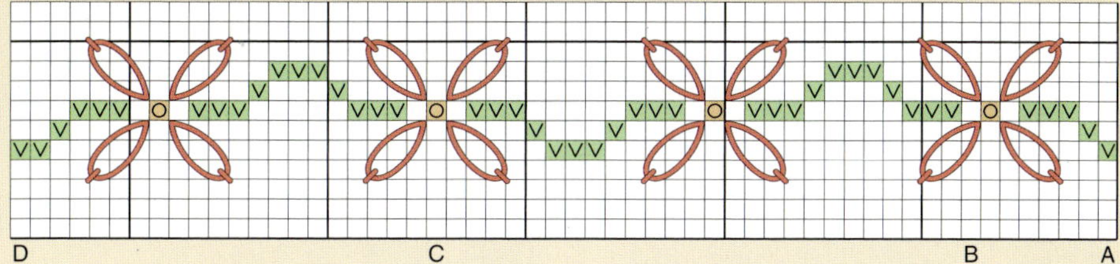

HAPPY KNIT HAT CHART

KEY
- White
- Gold Bobble
- Leaf Green Duplicate Stitch
- Rich Red Lazy Daisy

Knitting Abbreviations

Beg - beginning
BO - bind off
CO - cast on
Cont - continue
Dec - decrease
Dpn - double-pointed needles
Est - established
Inc - increase
K - knit
K2tog - knit next two stitches together
MB - make bobble
P - purl
Pat - pattern
Rem - remaining
Rep - repeat
Rnd(s) - round; rounds
RS - right side
St st - stockinette stitch
St(s) - stitch; stitches
WS - wrong side
Yb - yarn back
Yo - yarn over

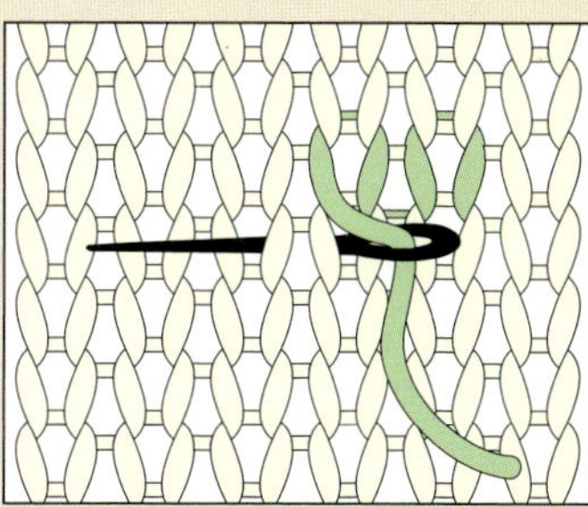
DUPLICATE STITCH

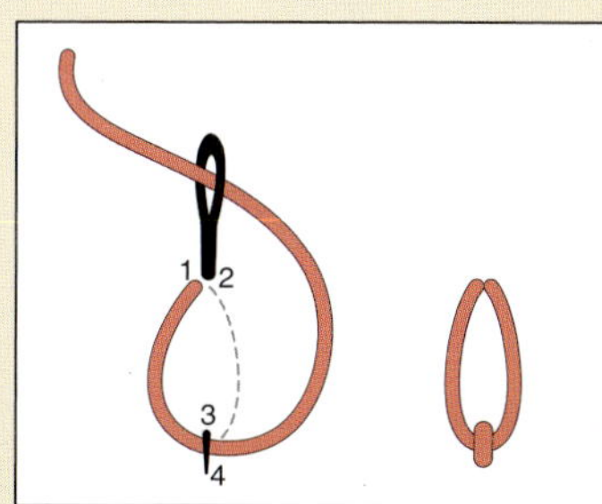

LAZY DAISY

SNOW FELLOW FRIEND

Adapted from Mary's paper garland design, this cuddly fleece character is small enough to hold in your hand and will surely melt your heart.

WHAT YOU'LL NEED

Tracing paper; pencil; scissors
8x16-inch piece of white fleece
Pins
Cotton embroidery floss in orange, black, red, and green
Two 5mm black beads for eyes
Three ¼-inch heart buttons
3x8-inch piece of black felt
Plastic bead pellets
Felt in yellow and green
¼-inch blue button
5-inch piece of ¼-inch-wide red-and-white polka-dot ribbon
Red thread; powder rouge

HERE'S HOW

1 Enlarge and trace the patterns, *right,* onto tracing paper. Layer the fleece with wrong sides facing. Pin the snowman pattern onto the fleece. Machine-stitch around the snowman, leaving an opening at the top of the head. Cut out close to stitching.

2 Satin-stitch (see *page 191*) nose using two plies of orange floss. Work black French knots, *page 190,* for mouth. Sew on black beads for eyes. Sew heart buttons down the center of the tummy. Using the hat pattern, cut out two black felt hat pieces. Stitch along sides and top, close to the edge. Pour pellets into the body. Baste the opening closed.

3 Pin hat onto head. Topstitch through all layers.

4 Use patterns to cut a yellow circle and two green holly leaves from felt. Add a center vein to each leaf using green floss and a straight stitch. Layer and sew holly leaves, yellow circle, and blue button to ribbon with red floss, positioning them so the flower will show on the front of the hat. Tack ribbon above hat brim using tiny stitches. Blush cheeks with powder rouge.

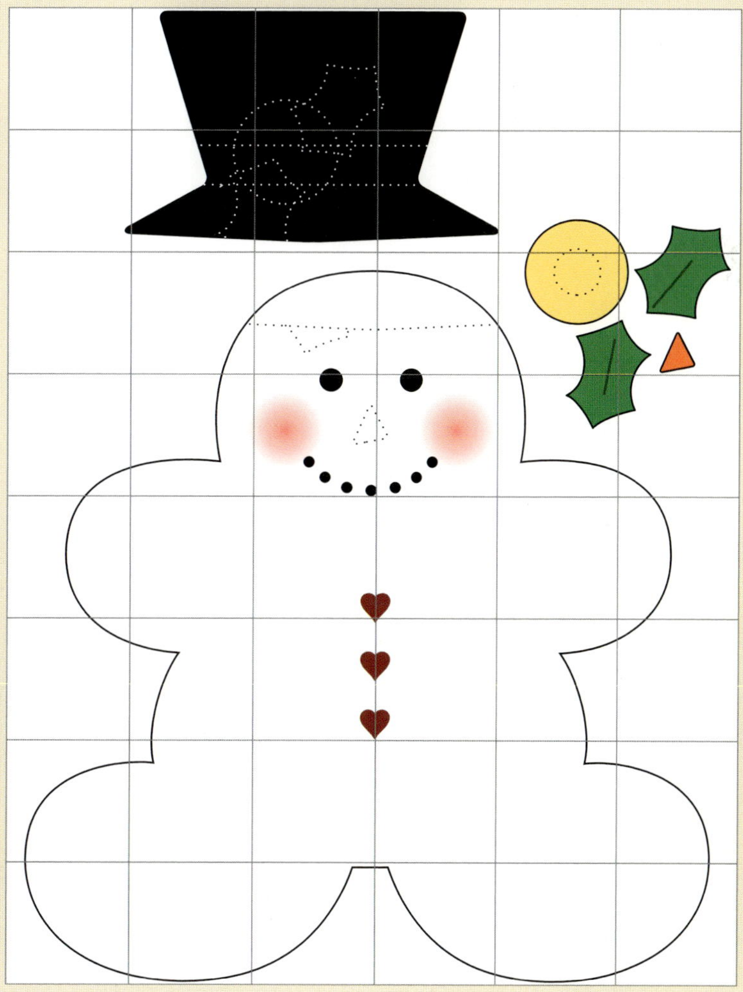

SNOW FELLOW FRIEND PATTERNS 1 SQUARE = 1 INCH

PRETTY FAUX PACKAGES

Under the tree or as a centerpiece, these merry packages add to the lure of gift-giving. The fabric-covered blocks can be used year after year.

WHAT YOU'LL NEED

Wood blocks in desired sizes
Fleece by the yard
Spray-mount glue for craft projects
Calico fabrics cut as fat quarters (18×22 inches) purchased at quilt shops, or ¼ to ½ yards of fabric
Fusible transweb paper
Assorted ribbons

HERE'S HOW

1 Using a wood block for the pattern, cut a fleece piece for each side of the block. Attach the fleece to the block using spray-mount glue. Smooth the fleece onto the block.

2 Cut calico fabrics to fit blocks, allowing enough fabric at ends to fold in package fashion. Use transweb paper to fuse fabric at seams and folded ends of fabric. Add ribbons and bows as desired.

ELF POCKET PLACE MATS

As cute as the pants on Mary's elf, this playful place mat has zigzag trimmed pockets—ready to present a holiday napkin and silverware.

WHAT YOU'LL NEED

½ yard of green corduroy
Fabric marking pencil; ruler
½ yard of batting
Green rayon machine embroidery thread
Tracing paper; pencil
½ yard of lining fabric
2 yards of red piping
#5 pearl cotton in green and gold
⅛ yard of gold imitation suede
⅛ yard of red felt; pinking shears
2 red 1½-inch buttons

HERE'S HOW

1 Cut a 16×34-inch piece of green corduroy. Trim angles on short ends as shown in the photo, *below.* Mark fabric in a 1-inch diamond grid. Line with batting. Machine quilt on grid using rayon thread.

2 Enlarge and trace the patterns, *below.* Cut the following, adding seam allowance:

- one lining (same as quilted corduroy) from lining fabric
- two pocket shapes (one in reverse) from quilted corduroy
- two pocket linings (one in reverse)
- two gold imitation suede pocket trims (one in reverse)
- two red felt pocket trim (one in reverse) with pinking shear edge
- red felt 1¼×15-inch band with pinking shear edge

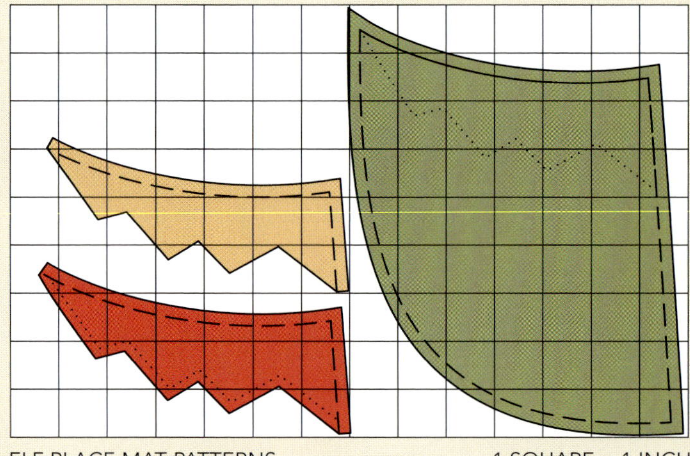

ELF PLACE MAT PATTERNS 1 SQUARE = 1 INCH

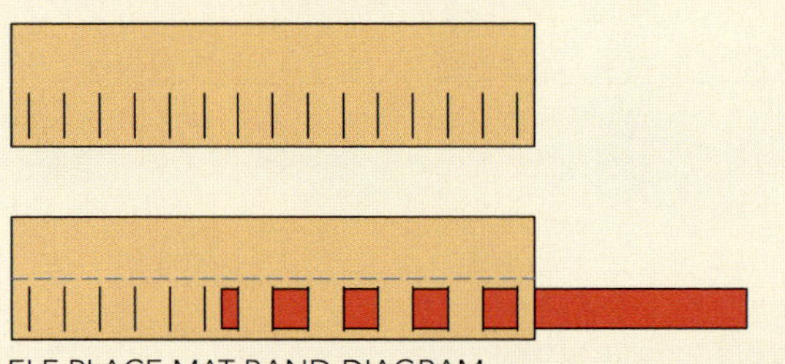

ELF PLACE MAT BAND DIAGRAM

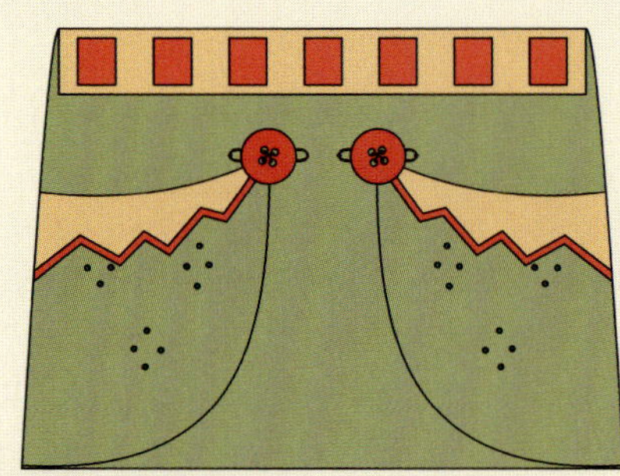

ELF PLACE MAT SCHEMATIC

- $3\frac{1}{2}$×15-inch piece of gold imitation suede with pinking shear edges

3 Topstitch the two pocket trim pieces together in pairs as shown, *above,* along the zigzag shape. Stitch pocket trim along top edge of pocket, right sides facing. Stitch pocket lining to pocket along top and curved edges. Clip seam. Turn to right side. Baste raw side edges together as side seam of place mat. Topstitch curve of pocket to place mat.

4 Stitch red piping along the sides and the bottom edge of place mat. Stitch the lining fabric on the piping line. Trim and clip seam. Turn through top edge. Baste top edges together.

5 Make scant $1\frac{1}{4}$-inch slits, 1 inch apart, vertically along one long side of the gold suede band. Weave red felt strip through slits. Bind top edge of place mat with band. With gold pearl cotton, make a large lazy daisy stitch, *page 190,* on each side of button placement. Repeat with another slightly larger lazy daisy stitch. Sew on buttons with gold pearl cotton. Using green pearl cotton, trim pockets with several sets of French knots, *page 190,* in diamond shapes.

HOLIDAY SHOPPING TOTE

Sturdy enough for shopping or for delivering holiday packages, this festive quilted bag will make it impossible to pout, much like Mary's card.

WHAT YOU'LL NEED

Scissors
1 yard of red print fabric
1⁄3 yard of blue print fabric
1½ yards of lining fabric
1½ yards of fleece
1 yard of ¼-inch twisted red-and-gold cord for handle
Tracing paper; pencil
8×8-inch piece each of green velveteen and two shades of green corduroy for trees
Fusible transweb paper
Scrap of brown fabric for tree trunks
¼ yard of green print for grass
1½ yards of red piping
Rayon thread for machine embroidery
35 green faceted 8mm beads
48 white 1¼-inch star appliqués
48 crystal flower beads
48 crystal 5mm seed beads

HERE'S HOW

1 Stitch with ¼-inch seams and right sides facing, unless otherwise indicated. Cut the following sashing strips from the red print or indicated fabric:

- Four strips for top and bottom of center panel – 2½ inches wide and 12½ inches long for front and back
- Four sashing strips for top and bottom of end panels – 2½ inches wide × 3 inches long
- Eight side sashing strips for each panel – 2½ inches wide × 13½ inches long
- Cut one blue front panel for design background – 9½ inches ×12½ inches
- Cut one red print back panel – 9½×12½ inches
- Cut two red print end design panels – 9½×3½ inches
- Cut lining and fleece side pieces – 13½×46½ inches
- Cut red print bottom, lining, and fleece bottom – 16½×7½ inches

Cut two pieces of red and gold cord for handles, each 15 inches.

2 Trace and cut out the full-size patterns, *page 103*. For front and side panels, use tree patterns as a guide to piece fabrics for crazy patchwork. Piece together three fabrics large enough for tree shapes. Trace tree shapes onto transweb paper. Fuse to wrong side of patchwork, and cut out. Trace, fuse and cut out tree trunks from brown. Trace, fuse and cut out green print for grass sections, allowing seam at sides and bottom edge.

3 Using the placement diagram as a guide, place and fuse trees and trunks onto blue background. Place and fuse green grass onto background. With rayon thread, machine appliqué (a close zigzag) the trees, trunks, and grass. Hand- or machine-embroider a decorative stitch to detail patchwork on trees. Add green beads for trim.

4 Stitch top and bottom sashing strips to front, back, and side panels. Stitch a sashing strip to each side of front, back, and side panels. Fuse or hand-stitch star appliqués according to photo, *opposite*. Stitch sashing strips together at three corners. Line bag with fleece, and machine-quilt as desired. Stitch remaining corner of bag. Line and baste fleece to bag bottom. Stitch bottom of bag to sides. Stitch lining piece at side seam. Stitch bottom lining to side lining. Baste a handle to bag front and back 2½ inches in from corner seams. With right sides facing, sandwich piping between layers. Stitch lining to bag around top edge, keeping handles free and leaving an opening for turning.

5 Turn bag to right side through opening. Stitch opening closed. Press lining to wrong side. Add crystal flower beads with a 5mm crystal to centers of stars on bag front.

HOLIDAY SHOPPING TOTE *continued*

PLACEMENT DIAGRAM

SIDE 1 PANEL PLACEMENT DIAGRAM

SIDE 2 PANEL PLACEMENT DIAGRAM

HOLIDAY SHOPPING
TOTE TREE PATTERNS
TRUNK

GIFT TAG TRIO

Scraps of construction paper are cleverly transformed into holiday gift tags with graphic appeal. Turn the page for instructions and patterns.

GIFT TAG TRIO *continued*

WHAT YOU'LL NEED

for the tree tag

Construction paper in red, light blue, green, brown, and white
Ruler
Pencil
Scissors
Tracing paper
Crafts knife
Star paper punch
Glue stick

for the holly tag

Construction paper in white, royal blue, green, and red
Ruler
Pencil
Scissors
Tracing paper
Paper punches in small and large circles
Glue stick

for the bow tag

Construction paper in white, red, and green
Ruler
Pencil
Scissors
Tracing paper
Star paper punch
Glue stick

HERE'S HOW

1 *For the tree tag,* cut a 3¼×2¼-inch piece from light blue paper. Trace full-size patterns, *opposite,* onto tracing paper. Transfer the red frame, trees, and grass each to the appropriate color of paper. Cut out the shapes. On a protected surface, use a crafts knife to cut the red frame shape. Glue the red frame at the top of the tag. Add the grass and trees. Use a star paper punch to make 16 white stars. Glue in place using the pattern as a guide. Let the glue dry.

2 *For the holly tag,* cut a 2¾×5¾-inch piece from white construction paper. Fold in half with the short ends together. Cut a 2¼-inch circle from royal blue paper. Glue in center of one side of the tag. Trace the holly pattern, *opposite,* onto tracing paper. Use pattern to cut two leaves from green paper. Fold in half lengthwise to form a center vein. Glue folds in leaves to the blue circle, ½-inch from the top, angling downward. Use a large paper punch to make three red dots. Use the same punch to punch crescent-moon shapes from white paper to add as highlights to the berries. Glue berries and highlights in place. Use a small paper punch to make approximately 18 circles from white. Glue randomly on the blue circle. Let the glue dry.

3 *For the bow tag,* cut a 6½×1½-inch piece from white paper. Fold in half with short ends together. From green, cut two ¼×1½-inch pieces for bow tails Notch one end of each bow tail. Cut two ¼×1-inch pieces for bow loops. Bring short ends together, and glue. Cut one ¼×½-inch piece for bow center. Glue short ends together to form a ring. Beginning with tails, glue to top of card near fold in an inverted V shape. Add the bow loops and the center ring to complete the bow. Use a star paper punch to make approximately 15 star shapes from red. Glue the star shapes randomly on the front of the card. Let the glue dry.

TREE TAG PATTERN

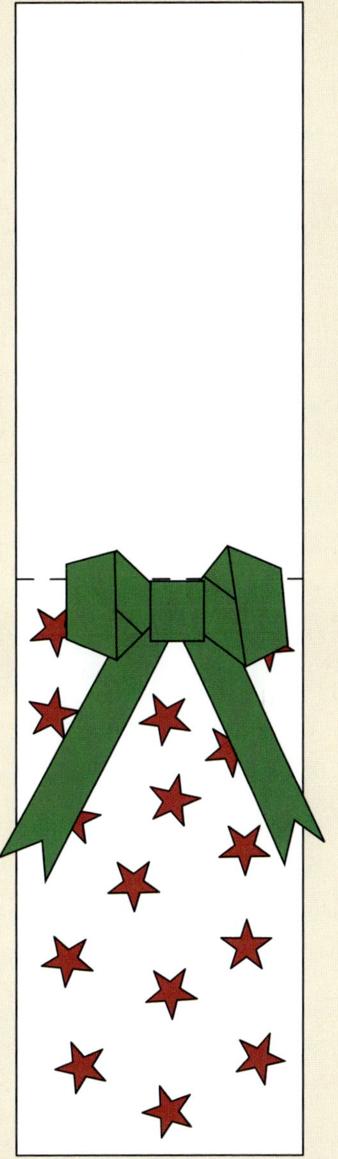

BOW TAG PATTERN

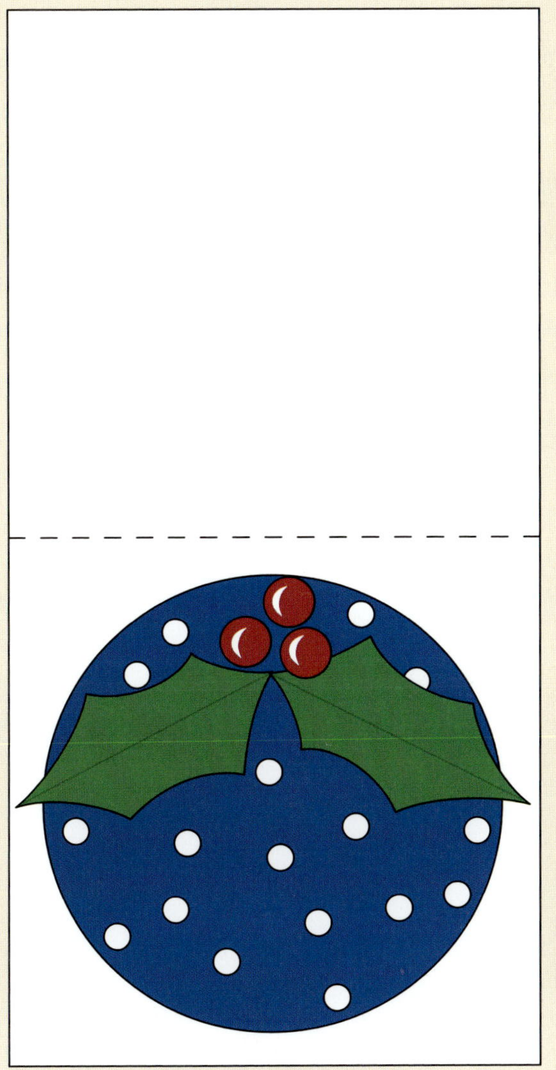

HOLLY TAG PATTERN

STARS 'N' CANDY CHECKERS

Ready to brighten up your holiday decor or to entertain those who are kids at heart, this charming game set is made from purchased wood shapes.

WHAT YOU'LL NEED

9×12-inch piece of routed pine
Sandpaper; ruler; pencil
Acrylic paints in black, red, royal blue, white, and yellow
Liner and flat paintbrushes
Tracing paper; 1-inch wood stars
¾-inch wood plugs
Black marking pen

HERE'S HOW

1 Sand wood piece smooth. Use a ruler to measure and mark an 8×8-inch square in the center of the board. Within the square, make a mark every inch. Connect the marks to create a 1-inch grid for the checkerboard.

2 Beginning in one corner, paint every other square white. Let dry. Paint the remaining squares black. Let dry.

3 Trace the full-size pattern, *below left*. Trace four scroll and heart patterns on each end of the game board.

4 Paint the inside border and hearts red. Paint the scrolls blue. Let the paint dry. Paint the remaining board black. Let dry.

5 To make white dots, dip the handle end of a paintbrush into paint, and dot onto the surface. Let the paint dry. To add highlights to the scroll, using a very small amount of white on a paintbrush, lightly brush the areas to be highlighted. Let the paint dry.

6 For the stars, paint the tops and sides yellow. Let the paint dry.

7 To make the peppermint game pieces, paint the plugs white. Let the paint dry. Use a liner paintbrush and paint five red lines on each plug to resemble a peppermint. Let the paint dry.

8 Use a marking pen to outline the checkerboard and define painted edges.

CHECKERBOARD PATTERN

CHECKERBOARD SCHEMATIC

EFORE CHRISTMAS

WOOL APPLIQUÉ STOCKING

Mimicking the coat on Mary's St. Nick, vivid wool shapes create striking contrast on this rich black, surprise-filled stocking.

WHAT YOU'LL NEED

Tracing paper
Pencil
Scissors
½ yard of black wool fabric
½ yard of fleece for lining
Fusible transweb paper
6×24-inch piece of red wool fabric
6×24-inch piece of blue wool fabric
6×6-inch piece of rose wool fabric
6×6-inch piece of green wool fabric
6×6-inch piece of gold wool fabric
3×3-inch piece of orange wool fabric
Pinking shears
Matching rayon thread for machine embroidery
Needle
#5 pearl cotton in rose, green, and red
Fabric glue
2 yards of purchased sew-in piping
Four ⅝-inch red heart buttons
Crochet hook
One 1-inch plastic ring for hanging loop
1 yard of ½-inch-wide black-and-white polka-dot ribbon

HERE'S HOW

1 Enlarge and trace the stocking pattern, *page 112.* Cut out the stocking front and back from black wool. Repeat with lining pieces.

2 Trace the full-size appliqué shapes onto transweb paper, and fuse to the corresponding wool fabrics. Cut out with regular scissors or pinking shears as indicated in the photo, *opposite.* Allow a scant amount of extra fabric where indicated on the pattern when one appliqué overlaps another.

3 Fuse the wool shapes to the stocking front following the manufacturer's instructions. Machine-appliqué (close zigzag or machine embroidery stitch) with matching threads, or straight-stitch appliqué pieces.

4 Line the stocking with fleece. Machine-quilt around appliquéd shapes as desired. Using pearl cotton, add French knots, *page 190,* where indicated in the photo, *opposite.*

5 Stitch piping along outside edge except at the top. Stitch stocking front to back. Trim and clip seam. Turn to right side. Stitch piping around top edge. Stitch lining pieces together leaving an opening for turning. Slip stocking into lining. Stitch around top edge. Pull stocking through lining opening. Stitch opening closed. Press lining to the inside.

6 Trim the shanks from the heart buttons. Using the placement diagram on *page 112* as a guide, glue hearts onto stocking for detail. With red pearl cotton, single crochet around a plastic ring. Hand-stitch the ring to the stocking for a hanging loop. Tie a ribbon through the loop.

STOCKING
continued

STOCKING PLACEMENT DIAGRAM

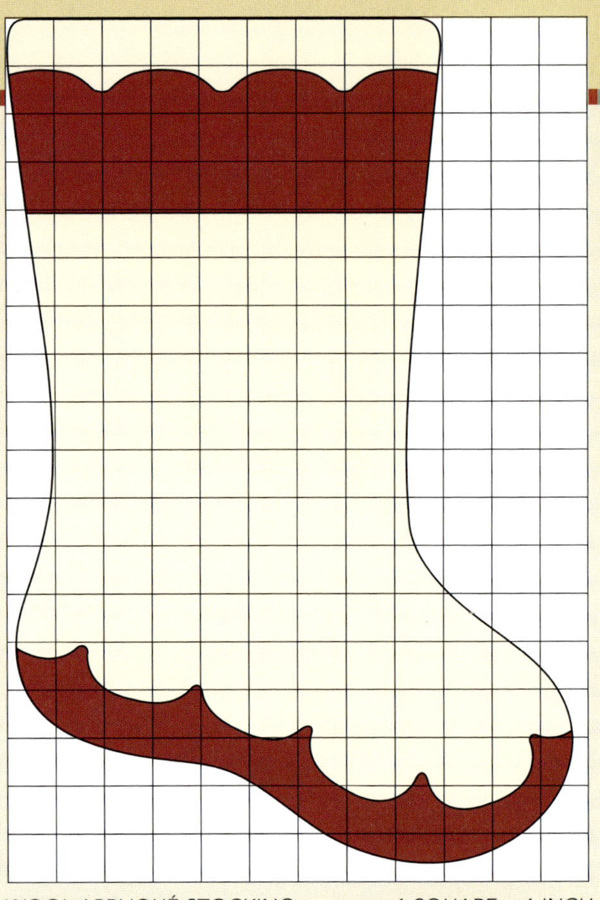

WOOL APPLIQUÉ STOCKING PATTERNS 1 SQUARE = 1 INCH

CUFF BORDER PATTERN

STOCKING BOTTOM PATTERN

SMALL FLOWER CENTER
PATTERN
FLOWER PATTERN
LEAF AND STEM
PATTERNS
TOE
EMBELLISHMENT
PATTERNS
LARGE FLOWER CENTER
PATTERN

JOY
for you!

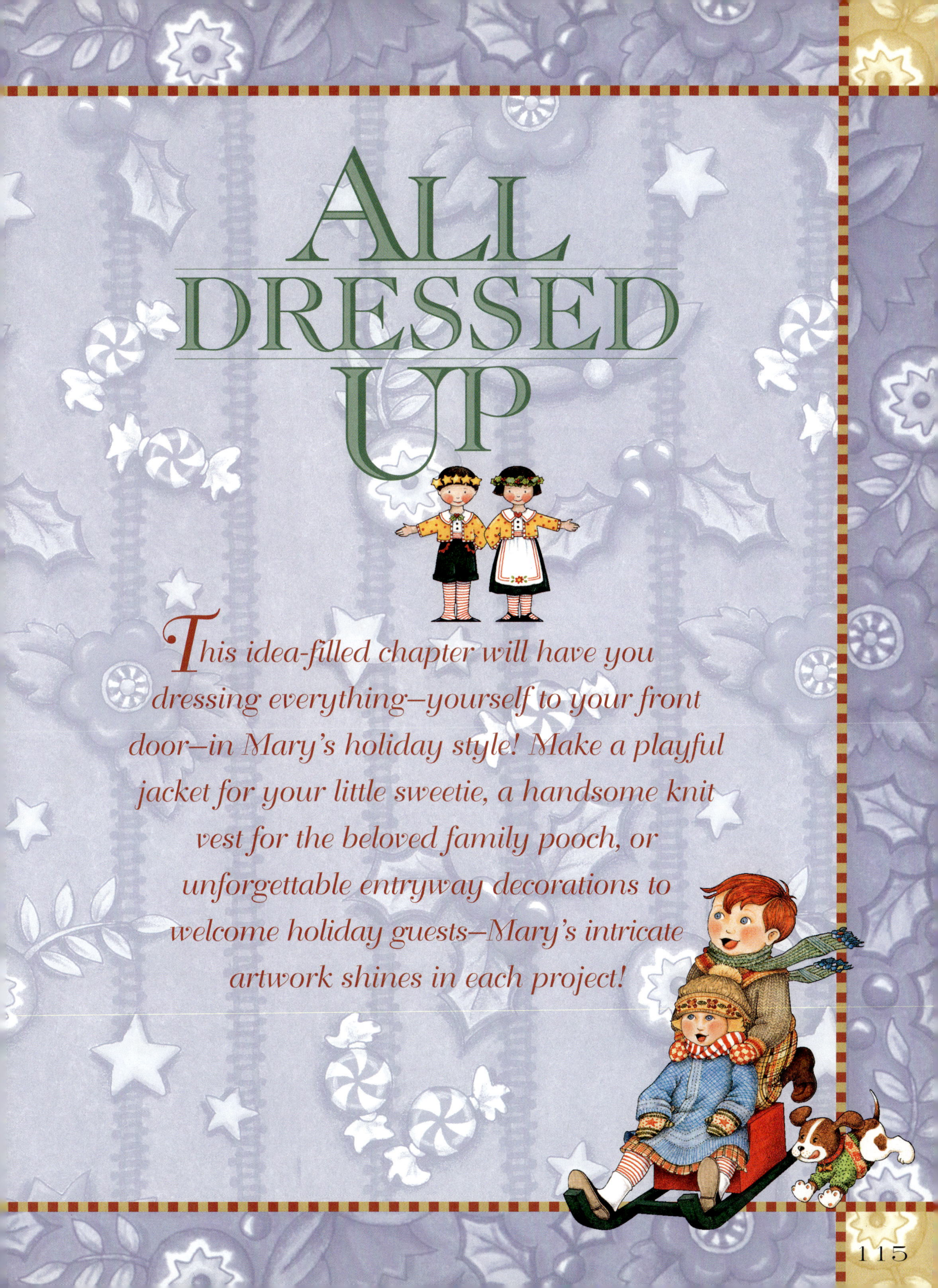

ALL DRESSED UP

This idea-filled chapter will have you dressing everything—yourself to your front door—in Mary's holiday style! Make a playful jacket for your little sweetie, a handsome knit vest for the beloved family pooch, or unforgettable entryway decorations to welcome holiday guests—Mary's intricate artwork shines in each project!

JOLLY JACKET

Your little princess will look sweet as an angel in this gold corduroy jacket trimmed with bright red buttons.

WHAT YOU'LL NEED
for the jacket

Scissors
For child's size 3, Burda pattern #3179 or similar pattern
1¼ yards of gold corduroy
1¼ yards of red lining fabric
Lightweight fusible interfacing
Approximately 32 red ¾-inch shank buttons
2½ yards of red-and-white stripe sew-in piping; thread

HERE'S HOW

1 Cut out jacket front, back, and sleeves according to the pattern instructions. Repeat for the lining. Omit the jacket facings and buttonhole closure.

2 Cut the interfacing from the back neck and front facing patterns. Fuse to the jacket.

3 Using the photograph, *opposite*, as a guide, sew red buttons on the sleeves, fronts, and back.

4 Assemble the jacket according to the pattern. Repeat with the lining.

5 Stitch piping around the outside edge of the jacket and at the sleeve hem. With right sides facing, stitch lining to jacket around outside edge, leaving an opening for turning. Trim and clip seams; turn. Stitch opening closed. Hand-stitch the sleeve lining to the sleeve hem.

WHAT YOU'LL NEED
for the pin

Tracing paper; pencil; scissors
Felt in red and green
Cotton embroidery floss in red and green; needle; pin back

HERE'S HOW

1 Trace patterns, *below*. Cut heart from red felt and holly leaves from green.

2 Work blanket stitches, *page 190*, around the outside edges using two plies of matching floss. Add straight-stitch veins in holly leaves. Stitch red heart to holly at center. Sew a pin back to the back of the holly leaves.

PIN HEART AND HOLLY PATTERN

BROTHER AND SIS DOLLS

These happy siblings, decked out in their holiday best, are cross-stitched on both the front and back sides.

WHAT YOU'LL NEED for one pair of dolls

Four 14×16-inch pieces of 28-count pink Jobelan fabric
Cotton embroidery floss as listed in key, pages 120 and 122
Needle
Fabric marking pencil
½ yard fleece
Thread
Poly-fil batting
Fabric glue
1½ yard gold flat trim for girl
1½ yard red flat trim for boy

HERE'S HOW

1 Tape or zigzag edges of the Jobelan fabric to prevent fraying. Find the center of the desired chart, *pages 120–123,* and the center of one piece of Jobelan fabric; begin stitching there. Use two plies of floss to work the cross-stitches over two threads of fabric. Work the other stitches as indicated in the key. Repeat for each remaining doll piece. Press the finished piece from the back.

2 Draw around the cross-stitched front pieces approximately ½ inch past the designs with a fabric marking pencil. Line the cross-stitch fronts and backs with fleece. Stitch together on the marked line.

3 *For each doll,* carefully match front to back with right sides facing. Stitch together around finished shape, leaving an opening at the bottom edge. Trim seam to ¼ inch. Clip seam. Turn to right side. Add poly-fil to shape doll. Stitch opening closed. Glue trim around doll on seam line. Let the glue dry.

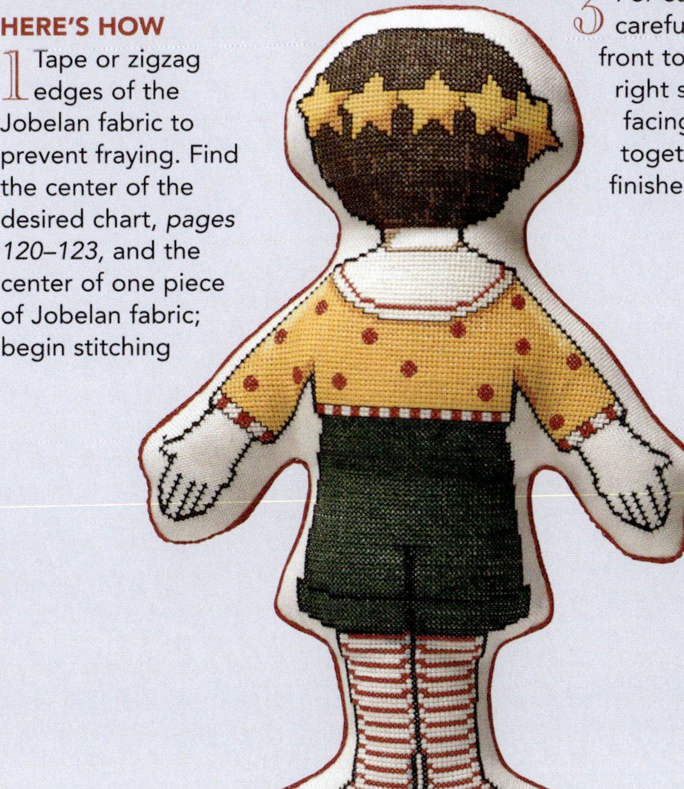

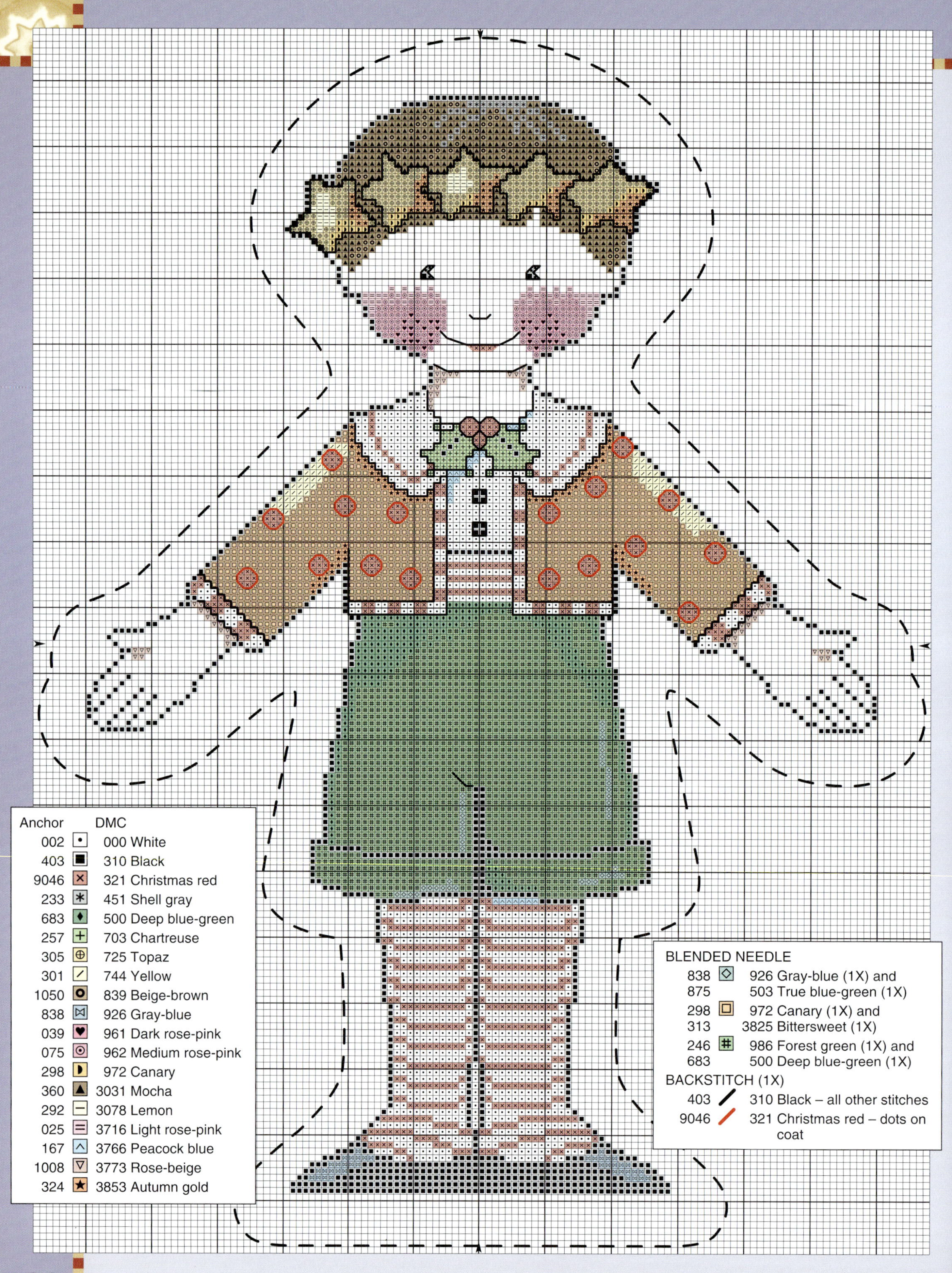

Anchor	DMC
002	000 White
403	310 Black
9046	321 Christmas red
233	451 Shell gray
683	500 Deep blue-green
257	703 Chartreuse
305	725 Topaz
301	744 Yellow
1050	839 Beige-brown
838	926 Gray-blue
039	961 Dark rose-pink
075	962 Medium rose-pink
298	972 Canary
360	3031 Mocha
292	3078 Lemon
025	3716 Light rose-pink
167	3766 Peacock blue
1008	3773 Rose-beige
324	3853 Autumn gold

BLENDED NEEDLE

Anchor	DMC
838 875	926 Gray-blue (1X) and 503 True blue-green (1X)
298 313	972 Canary (1X) and 3825 Bittersweet (1X)
246 683	986 Forest green (1X) and 500 Deep blue-green (1X)

BACKSTITCH (1X)

Anchor	DMC
403	310 Black – all other stitches
9046	321 Christmas red – dots on coat

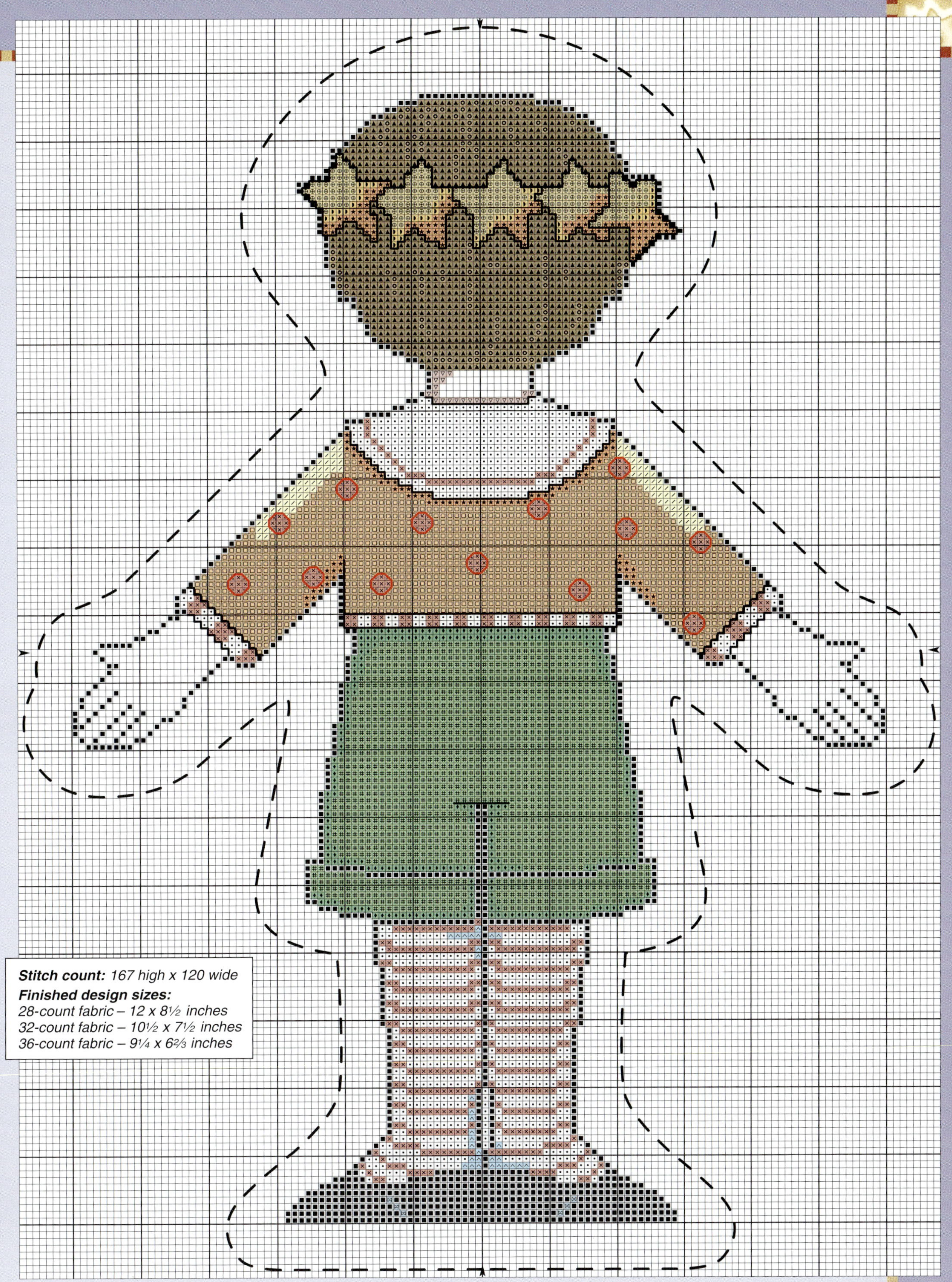

Stitch count: *167 high x 120 wide*
Finished design sizes:
28-count fabric – 12 x 8½ inches
32-count fabric – 10½ x 7½ inches
36-count fabric – 9¼ x 6⅔ inches

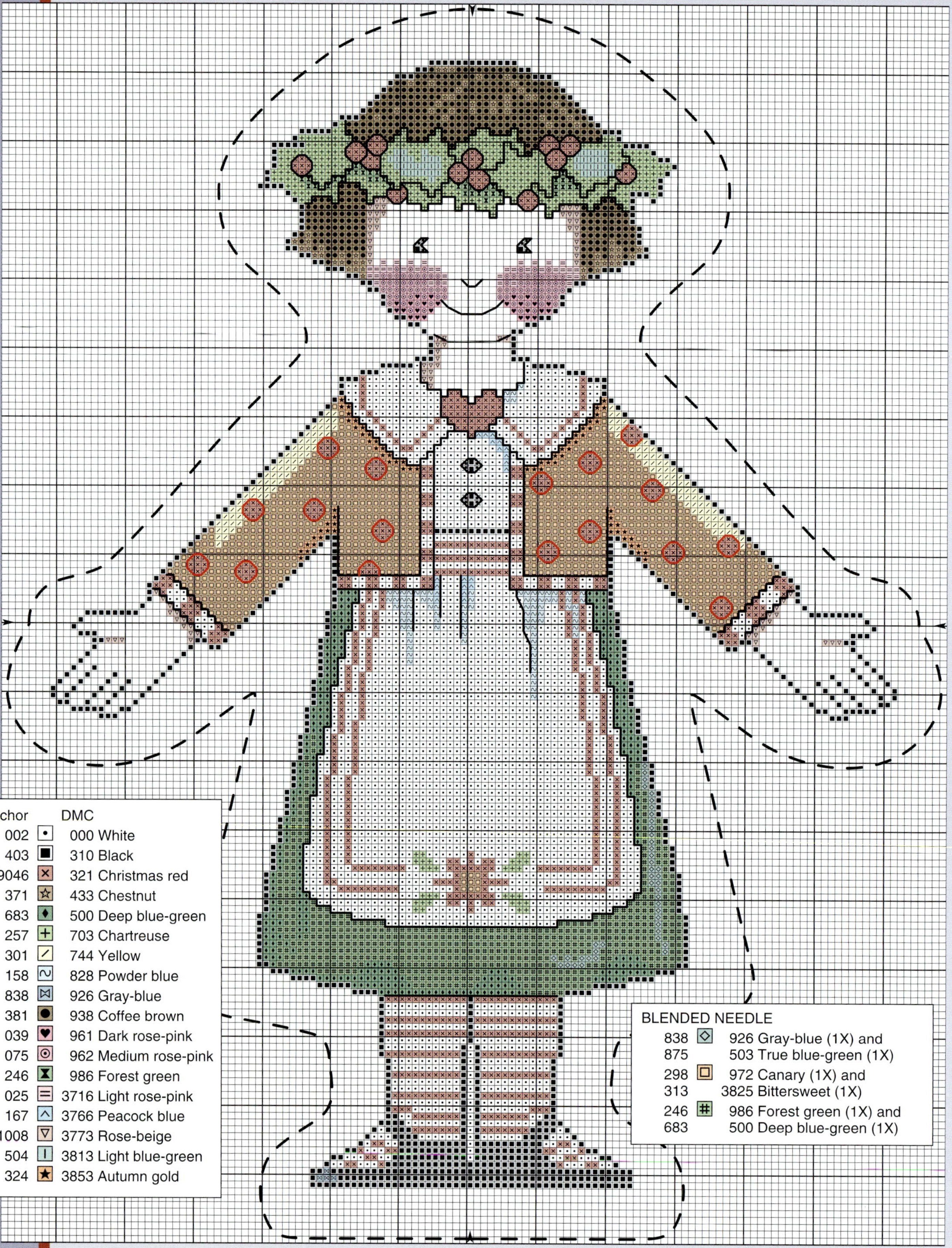

Anchor		DMC
002	•	000 White
403	■	310 Black
9046	✕	321 Christmas red
371	☆	433 Chestnut
683	♦	500 Deep blue-green
257	+	703 Chartreuse
301	/	744 Yellow
158	∾	828 Powder blue
838	⋈	926 Gray-blue
381	●	938 Coffee brown
039	♥	961 Dark rose-pink
075	⊙	962 Medium rose-pink
246	⧗	986 Forest green
025	=	3716 Light rose-pink
167	^	3766 Peacock blue
1008	▽	3773 Rose-beige
504	ǀ	3813 Light blue-green
324	★	3853 Autumn gold

BLENDED NEEDLE

Anchor		DMC
838 875	◇	926 Gray-blue (1X) and 503 True blue-green (1X)
298 313	□	972 Canary (1X) and 3825 Bittersweet (1X)
246 683	#	986 Forest green (1X) and 500 Deep blue-green (1X)

BACKSTITCH (1X)
403 310 Black – all other stitches
9046 321 Christmas red – dots on coat
Stitch count: *167 high x 120 wide*
Finished design sizes:
28-count fabric – 12 x 8½ inches
32-count fabric – 10½ x 7½ inches
36-count fabric – 9¼ x 6⅔ inches

HOLLY AND STARS CHRISTMAS PIN

A perfect gift or conversation piece for any Christmas party, this little clay pin—inspired by the border of Mary's card—also makes a wonderful ornament.

WHAT YOU'LL NEED

Waxed paper
Rolling pin
Bakeable clay, such as Sculpey, in black, white, red, green, and yellow
Round cookie cutter, approximately 2½ inches across
Cutting board; crafts knife
Baking dish
Glitter glaze; paintbrush
Large pin back
Clear silicone adhesive
½-inch-wide ribbon, optional

HERE'S HOW

1 Tear off two pieces of waxed paper, each approximately 12 inches long. Lay one piece on a hard, smooth work surface. Place the black clay in the center of the waxed paper. Place the remaining piece of waxed paper on top and press down on the clay with your hand.

2 Use the rolling pin to flatten the clay within the sheets of waxed paper. Roll out the clay until it is approximately ¼-inch thick. Remove the top layer of waxed paper.

3 Use a round cookie cutter to cut a circular shape from the black clay. Remove excess, and store in a plastic sandwich bag. Place the black cutout on a baking dish.

4 Roll out ⅛-inch coils of red and white clay. On a protected work surface, use a sharp knife to cut each of the coils into ¼-inch-long pieces.

5 Press the coil pieces along the edge of the black circle, alternating colors.

6 Mix a small amount of green and white clay. Blend slightly, but do not mix the colors completely. Place the green and white clay mixture between waxed paper sheets, and roll

PLACEMENT DIAGRAM

PATTERNS FOR HOLLY, STARS, AND BERRIES

out clay to a ⅛-inch thickness. Slide the waxed paper onto a cutting board. Use a crafts knife to cut three small holly shapes, using the patterns, *opposite*, as a guide. Roll out yellow clay in the same manner. Cut out two star shapes as shown, *opposite*, using a crafts knife. Following the placement diagram, *opposite*, press the holly leaves and stars onto the black clay circle.

7 Roll three pea-size balls from red clay. Press into place on the pin as shown, *above*. Using a tiny bit of white clay, make three crescent-moon shapes for the berry highlights. Press into place on each berry.

8 Roll 12 or more tiny white balls to make the background polka-dots. Carefully press the tiny balls onto the black areas between the holly and star designs.

9 Bake the assembled clay shapes in the oven according to the clay manufacturer's instructions. Remove from oven and let cool. Paint the stars with glitter glaze. Let the glaze dry. Glue a pin back at the top of the back of the piece. Let the glue dry. To make an ornament, pin the clay piece to a loop of ribbon.

Note: For tips on working with clay, see page 10.

DOGGY SWEATER

Protect your beloved pooch from winter drafts with this classy polka-dot bow-tie sweater.

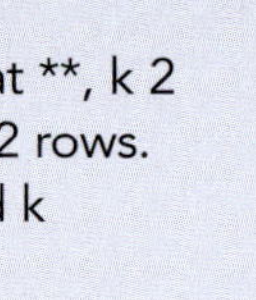

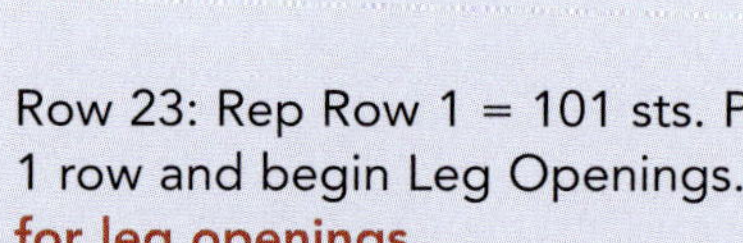

WHAT YOU'LL NEED

Patons Classic Wool, (223 yards/3½ oz. per skein): one skein each of Leaf Green (240), Forest Green (241), Old Gold (204), Rich Red (207)

Size 7 straight knitting needles or size to obtain gauge *below*

One set of size 7 double-pointed knitting needles (dpn)

HERE'S HOW

Gauge: In st st and color patterns, 20 sts and 26 rows = 4 inches.

Dog sizes: 1(2, 3, 4)

Chest: 8¼(10½, 13¾, 15½) inches

Length: 8½(9½, 10½, 12½) inches

Note: *When knitting with two colors in one row, carry the strand not in use loosely along the WS of the fabric. To change color, bring the next strand from under the present strand for a "twist" to prevent holes. Twist strands every 2–3 sts. Abbreviations are on page 191.*

Beginning at the neck with the straight needles and red, CO 41 (53, 69, 77) sts. K 2 rows. P 1 row. Bobble Row: K 2 with red; * make a bobble with leaf green [(9k in front and back of st) twice, slip second, third, and fourth sts over first st * bobble made (MB)] **, k 3 red; rep from * across ending last rep at **, k 2 red. With red, p 1 row, k 2 rows. Change to leaf green and k across. P 1 row.

for body (use leaf green with forest green bobbles)

Row 1 (RS): Inc 1 st each edge, k across.

Row 2: P 43(55, 71, 79) sts.

Row 3: Inc 1 st, k 2; * (MB, k 3) across, ending MB, k 2 inc 1 st = 45(57, 73, 81) sts.

Row 4 and each following WS row: Purl.

Row 5: Rep Row 1 = 47(59, 75, 83) sts.

Row 7: Rep Row 1 = 49(61, 77, 85) sts.

Row 9: Inc 1 st, k 3; (MB, k 3) across, ending MB, k 3, inc 1 = 51(63, 79, 87) sts.

Row 11: Rep Row 1 = 53(65, 81, 89) sts.

Row 13: Rep Row 1 = 55(67, 83, 91) sts.

Row 15: Inc 1 st, k 4: (MB, k 3) across, ending MB, k 4, inc 1 = 57(69, 85, 93) sts. For size 1 only, p 1 row and begin Leg Openings.

Row 17: Rep Row 1 = 71(87, 95) sts. For size 2 only, p 1 row and begin Leg Openings.

Row 19: Rep Row 1 = 89 (97) sts. For size 3 only, p 1 row and begin Leg Openings.

Row 21: Inc 1 st, k 1(MB, k 3) across, ending MB, k 1 inc 1 = 99 sts.

Row 23: Rep Row 1 = 101 sts. P 1 row and begin Leg Openings.

for leg openings

Work est pat on first 5(7, 8, 9) sts; BO 5(6, 8, 9) sts; work across next 37(45, 57, 65) sts, BO 5(6, 8, 9) sts. Place first and last 5(7, 8, 9) sts onto holders for later. Work 8(10, 14, 18) rows in est pat, ending with a WS row. Break yarn and place the sts onto a holder. With the RS facing, return the 5(7, 8, 9) sts to the left of the center to needle. Join leaf green and work 9(11, 15, 19) rows in est pat, ending with a WS row. Break yarn and return sts to a holder. With the WS facing, return rem 5(7, 8, 9) sts to needle. Join leaf green and work 8(10, 14, 18) rows in est pat, ending with a WS row. Rep est pat across next row and CO 5(6, 8, 9) sts. Rep est pat on 37(45, 57, 65) sts from holder; CO 5(6, 8, 9) sts, work est pat on rem 5(7, 8, 9) sts from holder. P 1 row on the 57(71, 89, 101) sts. Leaving long tails to weave in later, cut greens.

for chart

With the RS facing, using gold and red as shown on the chart, *left,* begin at #2(#3, #2, #1) and work to B. Rep A-B across, ending last rep at #5(#4, #5, #6). Complete the chart.

for ribbing (change to leaf green)

Row 1 (WS): (P 1, k 1) across ending p 1.

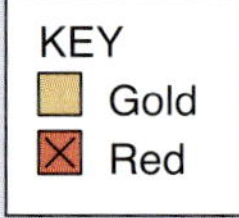

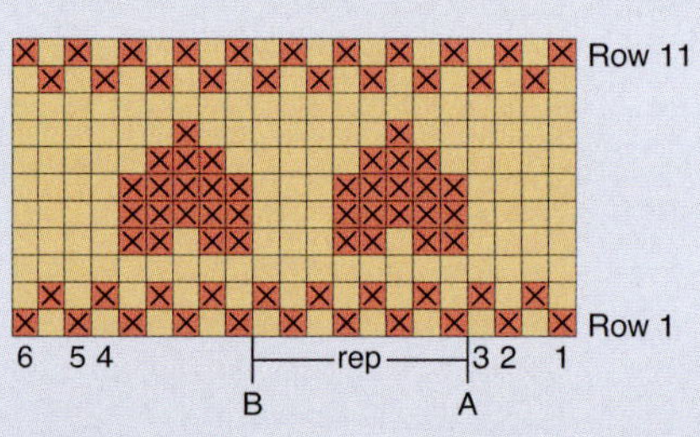

HEART CHART

Row 2: (K 1, p 1) across ending k 1. Rep rows 1–2 to 2(2½, 2½, 3)" from beg, ending with a WS row. BO in ribbing.

for leg cuffs (make two)

With the RS facing using dpn and leaf green, pick up and k 24(30, 42, 48) sts around leg opening. Arrange sts so there are 8(10, 14, 16) on each of 3 needles. Work around and around in k 1, p 1 ribbing until cuff measures 3 inches from beg. BO in ribbing. Turn back cuff.

for finishing

Using matching colors, sew center seam. Weave in loose ends on WS of fabric.

for bow tie

With red, CO 7(9, 11, 13) sts. Rep rows 1–2 of ribbing (see above) for 7(8, 9, 11) times. Rep Row 1 again. BO in ribbing. Weave in loose ends on WS of fabric. Cut a 10-inch strand of red. Fold the tie in half with the WS out to find the center. Wind the strand several times tightly around the center of the tie; tie in a square knot. Use the ends of the strand to secure to the underside of the sweater just below the neckband and centered over the seam.

BLACK VELVETEEN BONNET

Update an old-fashioned bonnet with flowers created from circles of colorful felt.

WHAT YOU'LL NEED

Pencil; ruler; scissors
Simple hat or bonnet pattern with no brim or bill
½ yard of black velveteen
½ yard of black lining fabric
½ yard of lightweight cotton fabric for underlining
Tracing paper
9×12-inch piece of felt in each of the following colors: pink, burgundy, purple, light blue, medium blue, teal, orange, and peach
9×12-inch pieces of felt in three shades of green
9×12-inch pieces of felt in two shades of gold
Matching colors of embroidery floss
Scraps of batting
1 yard of sew-in red-and-white piping
1 yard of cording for ties; thread

HERE'S HOW

1 Mark the hat pattern with a horizontal line from front, along the side, and toward the back about 3 inches down from top of head. Cut pattern on this mark. Cut out hat pieces from velveteen, adding ½-inch seam allowance to both sides of pattern cutting. This will allow a placement line for stitching piping to hat.

2 Cut lining pieces according to the pattern.

3 Trace and cut out the patterns, *below*. Use patterns to cut felt circles and leaves as shown in the photograph, *opposite*. Arrange and pin circle flowers and leaves onto velveteen. Allow a slight overlap of some flowers and leaves. Trim the excess from the inside curve of leaves where necessary. Trim excess from flowers in the seam allowance.

4 With two plies of embroidery floss in matching colors, work blanket stitches, *page 190*, around the circles and leaves. Stem-stitch veins of leaves with green floss. Add gold centers to flowers using blanket stitches adding a small amount of batting to shape the flower centers.

5 Finish the hat according to the pattern, adding piping in the seams. Add cording at the front edge for ties.

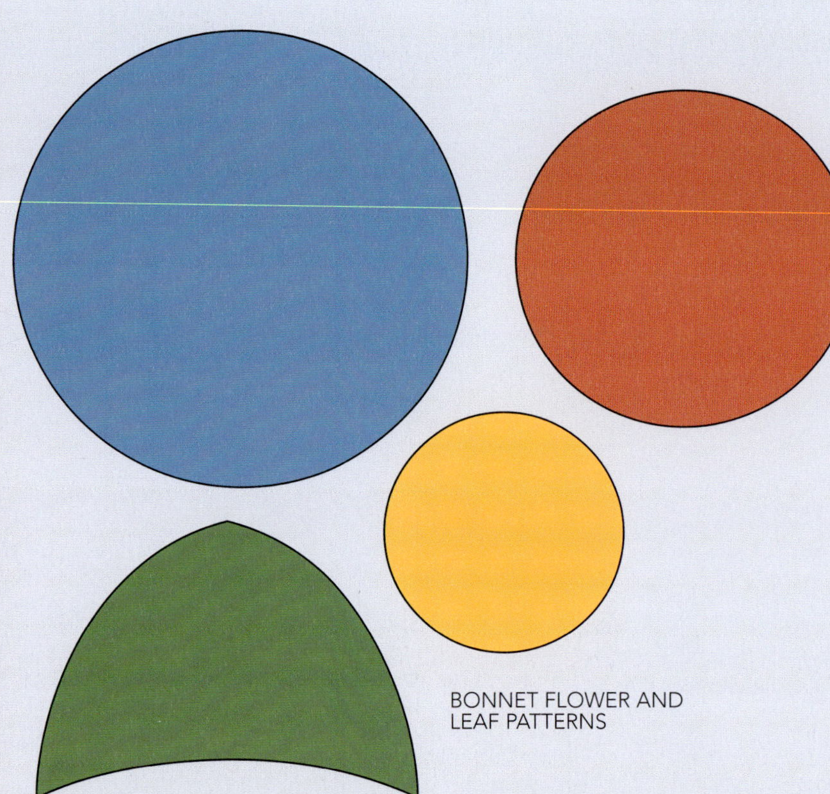

BONNET FLOWER AND LEAF PATTERNS

KNIT MITTS

Mary's art captures the joy of wintertime play. These darling mittens will keep hands toasty warm for countless outdoor adventures.

WHAT YOU'LL NEED

for one pair

Lambs Pride Superwash Bulky (100-gram or 110 yard skein): one skein of Turf Green (SW64) or Red Wing (SW01) plus Corn Silk (SW13) for contrast

Size 3 and 5 double-pointed knitting needles (dpn)

Yarn needle

2 small stitch holders

Stitch marker

1¼-inch red star appliqué

48 small red pony beads

HERE'S HOW

Gauge: Working in rounds of stockinette stitch (st st) and with large dpn, 5 sts and 7 rnds = 1 inch.

Children's size sm(med, large)

for mittens (make two)

With smaller dpn and main color, cast on 28(32, 36) sts. Arrange the sts onto 3 dpn; join and place a marker to indicate beginning of rnd. Work around in k 1, p 1 ribbing for 2(2½, 2½) inches.

Change to larger dpn. Knit every rnd for st st until the piece measures 2¾(3½, 3½) inches from beginning.

for thumb

Slip 6 sts onto holder; cast on 6 sts, k around = 28(32, 36) sts. Work even to 4¾(6, 6½) inches from beginning.

* For shaping, Rnd 1: (K 2, k2tog) around. Rnd 2: K 21(24, 27) sts. Rnd 3: (K 1, k 2 tog) around. Rnd 4: K 14(16, 18) sts. Rnd 5: (K2tog) around = 7(8, 9) sts. Cut yarn leaving an 8-inch tail. Thread tail into needle and back through remaining sts. Pull up to gather, and close top opening. Secure.

To complete thumb, k 6 sts from holder, pick up and k 6 more sts around opening. Arrange the 12 sts onto 3 dpn; join. Work around in st st until thumb measures 1¼(1½, 1¾) inches from beginning. K2tog around. Leaving a 6-inch tail, cut yarn. Thread tail into needle and back through remaining sts. Close opening and secure in place.

Work mittens according to specific instructions.

for red checked mittens

** (k 4 cream, k 4 red) for 1(2, 2) times, k 4 cream for 1(0, 0) times. *With next color k 1, with next color k 1; rep from * across palm. Rep from ** for 3 times more, working cream over red and red over cream on the palm. Alternating the checks with opposite colors and working tweed as est, work 4 rows. Cont as est, working thumb and top shaping with red.

for green striped mittens

In sm and med work 2 rounds of green after ribbing, then 2 rounds cream; 2 rounds green; 9 rounds cream; 2 rounds green; 2 rounds cream. Complete mitten and shaping in green. For thumb work 4 rounds of green then 3 rounds cream; complete thumb and shaping in green. For large mittens work 4 rounds of green after ribbing then work stripes as for sm and med. To detail center cream stripe, add a 1¼-inch purchased red star applique and 10 to 12 small red pony beads on each side of the star.

POLKA-DOT COAT

Make this a holiday to remember for your little one. Dress her up in this so-cute coat embellished with fake fur and big, bold polka dots.

WHAT YOU'LL NEED

McCalls Pattern #2410 size 4 or similar pattern (the jacket pattern was used, lengthening the hem several inches to the desired length)
Scissors
Red wool fabric and lining according to pattern with length adjustments
Fusible transweb paper
¼ yard of white fleece for dots
Press cloth
Thread
3 yards of 2-inch-wide white fake fur trim for cuffs and hem
½ yard of 4-inch-wide fake fur trim for collar
Five large snaps
5 green 1⅝-inch sew-through buttons
Green cotton embroidery floss
Needle

HERE'S HOW

1 Cut out the coat front, back, and sleeves according to the pattern, eliminating the facings. Repeat for the lining.

2 Trace approximately 25 circles onto transweb paper. Fuse to the white fleece. Cut out the fleece circles. Arrange the circles onto coat fronts, back, and sleeves. Lightly fuse the circles using a press cloth. Machine-zigzag around the circles.

3 Sew the coat front to the back, and set in the sleeves. Repeat for the lining. With right sides facing, stitch the coat to the lining along the front edges only. Trim and clip the seams. Turn to the right side. Top stitch down the center front on both sides. Baste the sleeve edge, neck edge, and hem edge to the lining on the seam line. Trim the seam allowance.

4 Bind the sleeves and hem the edge with 2-inch-wide fake fur trim. Bind the neck edge with 4-inch-wide fake fur trim.

5 Sew on snaps for the front closure. Using green embroidery floss, sew the buttons on the center front of the coat.

POLKA-DOT PATTERN

JOY

JOYOUS ENTRYWAY

Dress up your entry with a little holiday magic—a purchased post and painted wood cutouts that share the sentiments of the season—just like Mary's joyous doorway.

WHAT YOU'LL NEED for the plant stand

Deck or newel post; saw
Two 11¼-inch squares of 1½-inch-thick pine
Two 7¼-inch squares of ¾-inch thick pine
One 9½-inch square of ¾-inch-thick pine
Tracing paper; pencil; scissors
3⁄16-inch finished plywood
Scrollsaw; sandpaper
White spray primer
Acrylic paints in white, pale yellow, daffodil yellow, green, red, and black; paintbrushes
⅛- and ½-inch-wide red satin ribbon
Screws; thick white crafts glue
Ruler; pencil
3-inch wood star; drill with drill bit
Screw cup hook
Heavy crafting wire; wood glue

HERE'S HOW

1 If the bottom end of the post is notched, cut it off so it can stand on a flat bottom. If the post has a rounded top, cut it off so a board can be mounted on top.

2 The two 11¼-inch squares will be stacked at the bottom with a 7¼-inch square on the top of them. The 9½-inch square will be used for the top, with a 7¼-inch square underneath it.

3 Trace the flower pattern, *page 136,* onto tracing paper. Cut out and trace the pattern onto finished plywood. Cut out and sand until smooth. Make four for each post.

4 In a well-ventilated work area, prime each piece of wood with white spray primer. Let the primer dry.

5 Paint the large solid areas of the post first. Refer to the photograph, *left,* for color combinations and patterns. Paint each divided section of the post a different color or pattern.

To paint checks, use a small flat paintbrush. Paint white background first. Let dry. Paint in checks. To paint checks as on the base of our post, paint white first. Draw a square in the center of the 7¼-inch-square board the same size as the base of the post. Draw in pencil lines for checks, using a ruler and pencil. Then paint every other square using black. Let the paint dry. Paint the flowers and stars. Let the paint dry.

6 Glue and wind the wide ribbon around the smooth center of the post. Glue and wind the narrow ribbon between the wraps of the wide ribbon.

7 Drill a small hole at the top of the star. Cut an 18-inch

(continued on page 136)

JOYOUS ENTRYWAY *continued*

length of wire and wrap it around a pencil. Insert one wire end into the hole in the star. Curl the end up to secure. Form the opposite end into a loop. Drill a ¼-inch deep hole into one bottom corner of the stand top. Screw in a cup hook. Slip the wire loop from the star over the cup hook.

8 Assemble the stand using four screws at the bottom. Drill holes into sections, and secure with screws. Attach the top pieces using wood glue. Let dry.

WHAT YOU'LL NEED for the joy sign

Tracing paper; pencil; scissors
1½-inch-wide pieces of ½-inch thick wood: two 10½ inches long and two 28½ inches long
13½×28½-inch piece of ¼-inch-thick plywood
Scrap pieces of ½-inch-thick wood large enough to make letters
Scroll saw; sandpaper
White spray primer
Acrylic paints in red, white, black, yellow, and green
Black permanent marker
Wood glue; clamps
Bricks or heavy books
White screw cup hooks

HERE'S HOW

1 Trace the letters and holly onto ½-inch-thick wood. Cut out and sand the edges.

2 Prime all pieces with a white spray primer. Let dry.

3 On base board, draw in light pencil lines on all four sides 1½ inches in from the edges. Lay scalloped edge pattern down, centered along pencil line (scallops inward), and trace.

4 Paint inside background black and the scallops white. Paint letters yellow, berries red, and leaves green. To add subtle shading to the leaves, mix a little white with green. Put very little paint on the brush and make a few strokes onto scrap paper first. Very lightly paint with a dry brush technique onto one edge of the leaves. Brush back and forth, leaving a light highlight. Draw in leaf veins with a black permanent marker.

5 On the border strips, paint entirely white. Let dry. Mark off checks every 1½ inches. Paint in red on top and sides.

6 Glue on borders using wood glue. Hold in place with clamps while glue sets. Let dry.

7 Glue on letters and holly. It may help to weigh them down with items such as bricks or heavy books, placing a cloth between painted motifs and weights.

8 Screw in two white cup hooks on top edge.

JOY SIGN LEAVES PATTERN

JOY POST FLOWER PATTERN

JOY FRAME DIAGRAM

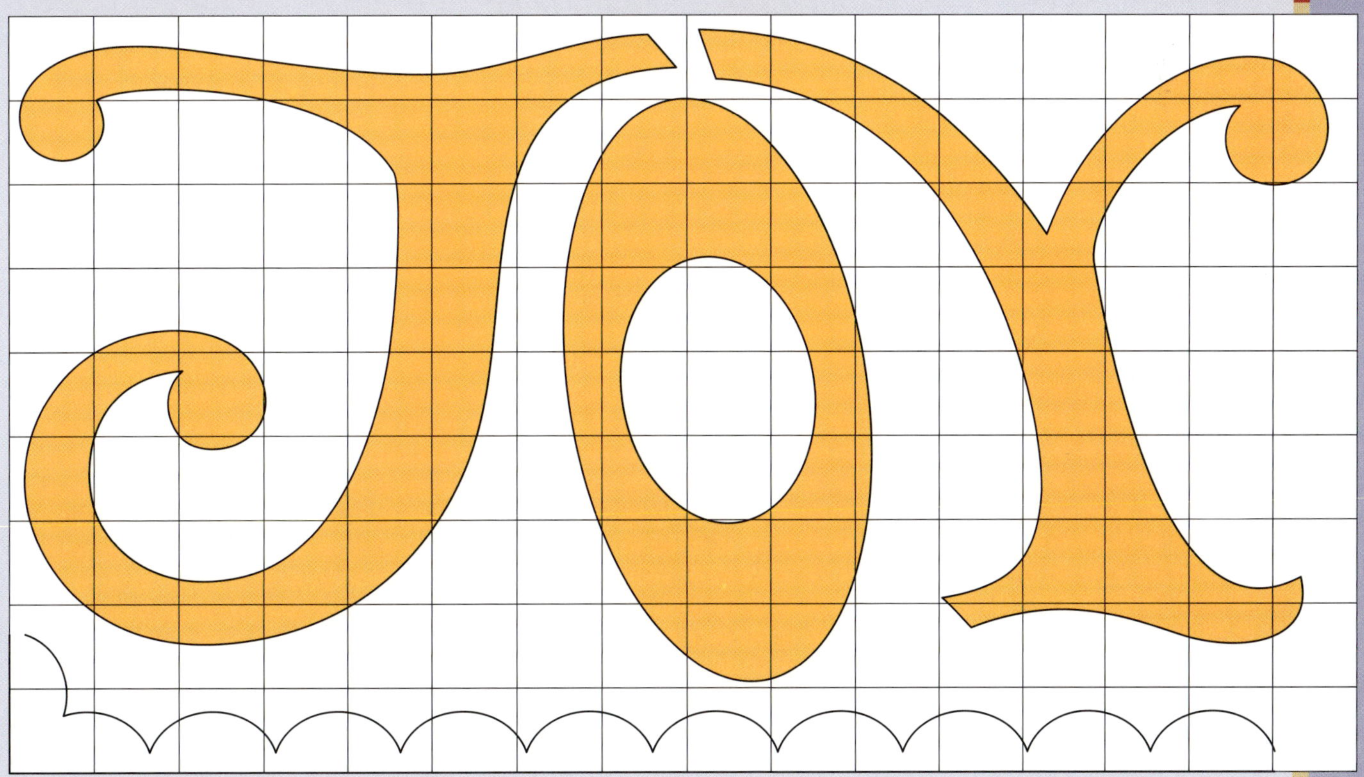

JOY LETTERING PATTERN

1 SQUARE = 1 INCH

HOLIDAY NECKLACE

With a spirited expression like the cookie on Mary's card, this gingerbread man is stitched on white Aida fabric and is embellished with tiny seed beads.

WHAT YOU'LL NEED

6×5-inch piece of 18-count white Aida fabric
Cotton embroidery floss as listed in key
Needle
Petite iridescent white glass seed beads
White thread; scissors
Fabric glue
4×3-inch piece of red imitation suede fabric; pinking shears
24-inch-long piece of red cord

HERE'S HOW

1 Find the center of the chart, *below,* and the center of the Aida fabric; begin stitching there. Use two plies of embroidery floss to work the cross-stitches over one square of the fabric. Work the other stitches as indicated in the key. Sew on seed beads using white thread.

2 Carefully trim around the stitched design, one square beyond the stitching. Center and glue the stitched piece atop the imitation suede piece. Let the glue dry.

3 Using pinking shears, trim the suede around the design. Glue the ends of the cord to the back side of the gingerbread man's head. Let dry.

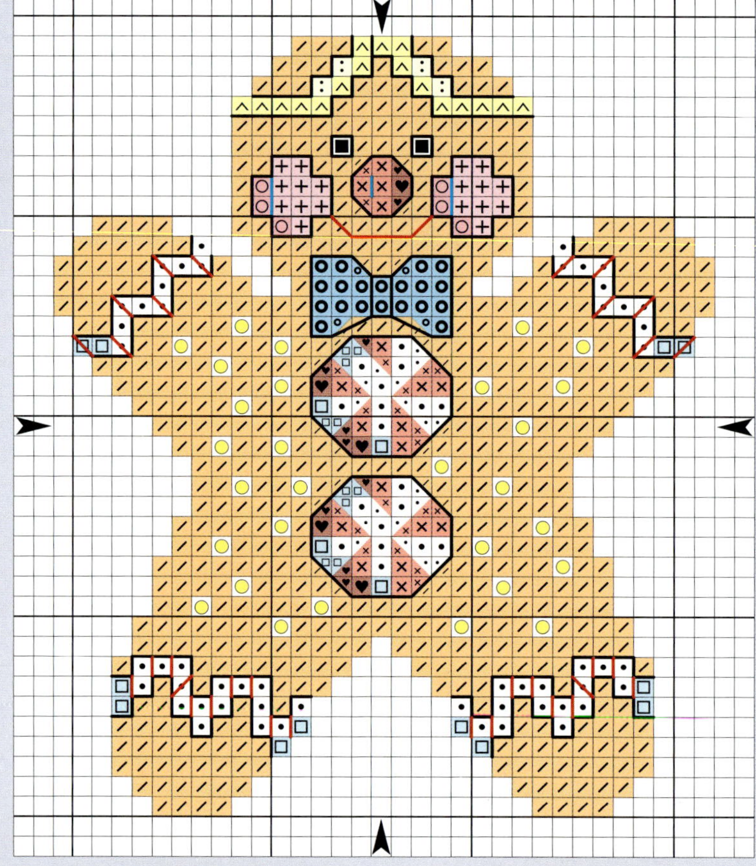

HOLIDAY NECKLACE PATTERN

Anchor	DMC
002	000 White
897	221 Shell pink
403	310 Black
9046	321 Christmas red
1038	519 Sky blue
063	602 Cranberry
305	725 Topaz
026	957 Geranium
386	3823 Yellow
410	3844 Bright turquoise

BLENDED NEEDLE

323	722 Bittersweet (1X) and
1002	977 Golden brown (1X)

BACKSTITCH (1X)

002	000 White – cheeks and nose highlights
403	310 Black – all other stitches
9046	321 Christmas red – icing stripes and mouth

MILL HILL BEADS

02058 White glass beads – sugar sprinkles

Stitch count: *39 high x 33 wide*

Finished design sizes:
18-count fabric – 2⅛ x 1⅞ inches
14-count fabric – 2¾ x 2⅜ inches
16-count fabric – 2½ x 2 inches

WINTER VEST AND EARRINGS

Feel as jolly as Mary's Santa wearing this festive vest or earrings set—sure to be a favorite all winter long.

WHAT YOU'LL NEED for vest

Vest pattern; pencil; tissue paper
¾ yard of blue boiled wool
24 strands of 30-inch-long three-ply white needlepoint wool yarn
½ yard of chartreuse green felt
Pinking shears
2½ yards of 1½-inch-wide flat heart trim for edge bands
5 yards of red/white narrow sew-in piping
¾ yard of red-and-white stripe flannel for piping
2 yards of ½-inch piping cord to be covered for armholes
2 yards of ½-inch-wide flat gold trim for armholes
2 yards of ¼-inch-wide gold trim for button loops
10 red-and-white stripe ¾-inch buttons; 20 gold 5mm beads

HERE'S HOW

1 Trace desired vest size pattern for front and back onto tissue paper. When working with boiled wool, use ¼-inch seams. Stitch right sides facing unless otherwise indicated. After stitching seam, topstitch ⅛-inch on each side of seam through garment and seam allowance. To eliminate bulk, omit lining and front, and neck facing.

2 Cut out vest front and back pieces. Mark vest front pattern piece into a 2-inch grid to determine placement of wool yarn detail. Re-mark vest front pattern piece with a 2-inch grid half way between first grid. Transfer marks to vest fronts.

3 To make yarn detail, work two straight stitches in "V" shape at the grid markings. Make another tiny straight stitch at the bottom of the "V".

4 Trace shape of front and bottom edge of vest front onto green felt. Using pinking shears, cut out a 2-inch-wide green felt band. Repeat for bottom edge of back. Topstitch heart trim to felt band while sandwiching red/white piping along edge of heart trim. Fold or pleat fullness of trim into corners. Topstitch bands to vest fronts. Stitch back seam of vest if needed, and topstitch band to bottom edge. Stitch vest front to back at shoulders.

5 Cut red/white stripe flannel on bias, and cover piping cord for armholes. Stay-stitch around armholes on seam line. Trim seam allowance. Topstitch arm hole edge to piping. Stitch gold flat trim over raw edge of armholes. Sew side seams. Stay-stitch around neck edge. Turn raw edge to wrong side, and top-stitch around neck edge. Evenly space and sew five buttons along band on vest fronts.

6 Cut ¼-inch-wide gold trim for button loops into five 12-inch pieces. Make a ½-inch loop at one end. Hand-tack to secure. Fold remainder of trim into a figure eight, hand-tacking ends together. Hand-tack at center crossing and again at ½-inch loop at opposite end.

7 Sew loops to right vest front. Sew a gold bead on each side of loops. Slip loops over buttons to close.

WHAT YOU'LL NEED for earrings

Tracing paper; pencil
Green crafting foam; scissors
⅞-inch white and ½-inch yellow buttons
Red acrylic enamel paint
Paintbrush; yellow embroidery floss
Earring backs; epoxy adhesive

HERE'S HOW

1 Trace leaf pattern, *below*. Use pattern to cut four shapes from green foam.

2 Paint six swirled red lines on each white button. Let dry.

3 Layer the buttons as shown. Sew together using yellow floss. Knot ends on the back.

4 Glue a pair of leaves on each earring. Glue on earring backs. Let the glue dry.

EARRINGS LEAF PATTERN

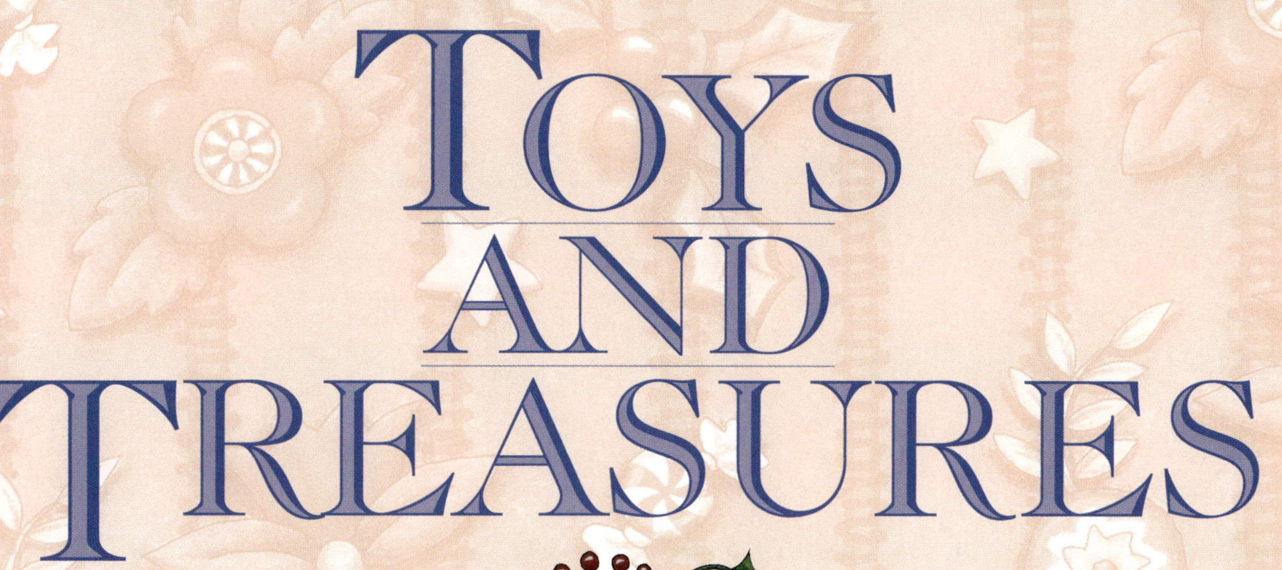

Fill your home with the excitement only Christmas brings. Crochet an adorable doll for your darling. Make a wood duck reminiscent of yesteryear. Cross-stitch a pillow that will be treasured for generations. Mary's holiday cards inspire wonderful Christmas gifts and decorations that brighten the holidays for family and friends.

“BELIEVE” SAMPLER

Cross-stitch this version of Mary's charming “Believe” illustration, and spread the magic of the jolly ol' soul. The chart is on pages 146–149.

WHAT YOU'LL NEED

18×22-inch piece of 28-count black Jubilee fabric
Cotton embroidery floss in colors listed in key
Embroidery hoop; needle
Beads as listed in key
Desired mat and frame

HERE'S HOW

1 Tape or zigzag the edges of the fabric to prevent fraying. Find the center of the chart, *page 146*, and the center of the fabric; begin stitching there. Use two plies of floss to work the cross-stitches and half cross-stitches over two threads of fabric. Work the remainder of the stitches using two plies unless otherwise noted in the key.

2 Press the finished piece from the back. Attach beads using one ply of matching floss.

3 Mat and frame the stitched piece as desired.

Anchor	DMC
002	000 White
1027	221 Shell pink
1006	304 Christmas red
403	310 Black
235	318 Steel
1025	347 Deep salmon
214	368 Pistachio
231	453 Light shell gray
862	520 Olive drab
063	602 Cranberry
239	702 Light Christmas green
256	704 Chartreuse
324	721 Bittersweet
303	742 Tangerine
1022	760 True salmon
132	797 Royal blue
379	840 Medium beige-brown
035	892 Carnation
326	900 Burnt orange
1012	948 Peach
1002	977 Golden brown
883	3064 Cocoa
1024	3328 Dark salmon
1048	3776 Mahogany
868	3779 Terra-cotta
236	3799 Charcoal
305	3821 Straw
386	3823 Pale yellow
013	3831 Dark raspberry
028	3832 Medium raspberry
159	3841 Baby blue
410	3844 Bright turquoise
311	3855 Autumn gold
341	3857 Dark rosewood
926	3866 Mocha

BLENDED NEEDLE

Anchor	DMC
231 / 378	453 Light shell gray (2X) and 841 True beige-brown (1X)
683 / 851	500 Blue-green (2X) and 924 Deep gray-blue (1X)
212 / 1076	561 Dark seafoam (1X) and 3847 Teal green (2X)
227 / 210	701 True Christmas green (2X) and 562 Medium seafoam (1X)
302 / 305	743 True yellow (1X) and 3821 Straw (2X)
379 / 233	840 Medium beige-brown (1X) and 451 Dark shell gray (2X)
897 / 341	902 Garnet (2X) and 3857 Dark rosewood (1X)
921 / 838	932 Antique blue (1X) and 926 Medium gray-blue (2X)
1044 / 403	934 Pine green (2X) and 310 Black (1X)
1044 / 683	934 Pine green (1X) and 500 Blue-green (2X)
242 / 239	989 Forest green (2X) and 702 Light Christmas green (1X)
382 / 403	3371 Black-brown (1X) and 310 Black (2X)
1019 / 1027	3802 Antique mauve (1X) and 221 Shell pink (2X)
013 / 028	3831 Dark raspberry (2X) and 3832 Medium raspberry (1X)
347 / 311	3856 Pale mahogany (1X) and 3855 Autumn gold (2X)
896 / 1019	3858 Medium rosewood (1X) and 3802 Antique mauve (2X)
926 / 001	3866 Mocha (2X) and 3865 Winter white (1X)

HALF CROSS-STITCH
(stitch in direction of symbol)

Anchor	DMC
235	318 Steel – stars

BACKSTITCH

Anchor	DMC
002	000 White – lettering, hat, boots, roof, chimney, window, bow on wreath, trees, beard
1006	304 Christmas red – lettering, flowers on coat, Santa, mouth, hobby horse, candy canes, Jack-in-the-box
403	310 Black – dog body, Santa eyes, candy, inner border
233	451 Dark shell gray – jacket fur
862	520 Olive drab – hobby horse stick
227	701 True Christmas green – candy, Jack-in-the-box, tree
132	797 Royal blue – roof, window
1041	844 Beaver gray – check pattern on coat
360	898 Coffee brown – duck, hobby horse, Santa features, house siding
242	989 Forest green – mittens
433	996 Electric blue – beard, candy
382	3371 Black-brown – all remaining stitches
305	3821 Straw – stars, ball
926	3866 Mocha – dog outline

STRAIGHT STITCH

Anchor	DMC
360	898 Coffee brown – teddy bear

BLENDED-NEEDLE STRAIGHT STITCH

Anchor	DMC
1006 / 002	304 Christmas red (2X) and 000 White (2X) – boot laces

COUCHING

Anchor	DMC
235	318 Steel – Christmas lights wire (3X)
433	996 Electric blue – hobby horse mane

FRENCH KNOT

Anchor	DMC
002	000 White – wreath in window
1006	304 Christmas red – flower centers on coat
403	310 Black – teddy bear, dog, Santa eyes
303	742 Tangerine – boot laces
382	3371 Black-brown – Jack-in-the-box mouth

MILL HILL BEADS

00479 White seed bead
40479 White petite bead

Stitch count: *234 high x 163 wide*

Finished design sizes:
28-count fabric – 16¾ x 11⅝ inches
32-count fabric – 14⅝ x 10⅛ inches
36-count fabric – 13 x 9 inches

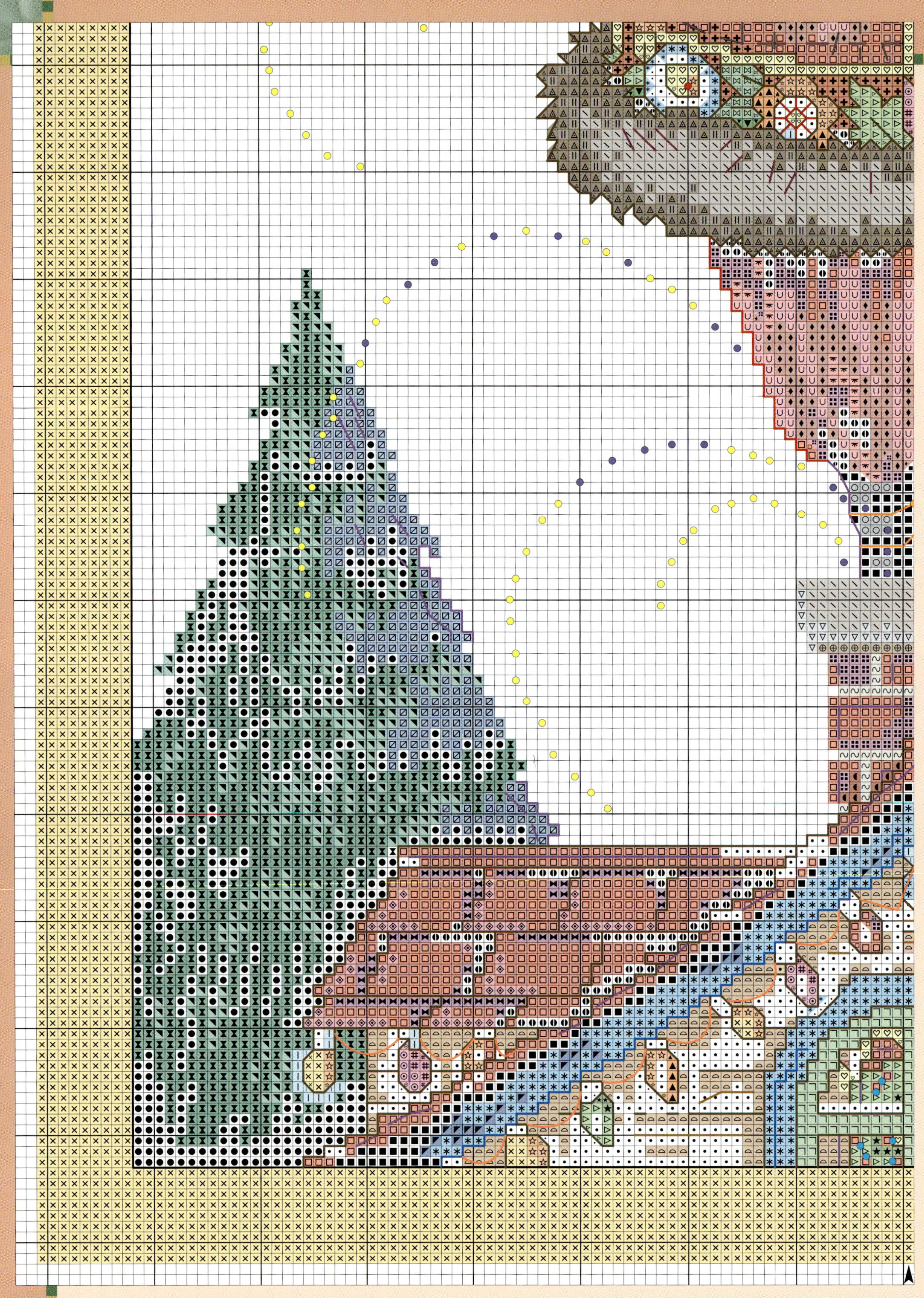

SCOTTY DOG PILLOW

Mary's Santa juggles a darling Scotty just like the holiday accent pillow we've created here.

WHAT YOU'LL NEED
Tracing paper
Pencil
Scissors
16×16-inch piece of black check wool
16×16-inch piece of red corduroy
1½ yards of white sew-in piping
Poly-fil batting
Embroidery floss in black and red
Needle; plaid dog novelty button
¾-inch white sew-through button
¼ yard of ½-inch red plaid ribbon
2 red jingle bells
2 green jingle bells

HERE'S HOW

1 Enlarge and trace the pattern, *below*, onto tracing paper. Use the pattern to cut out the

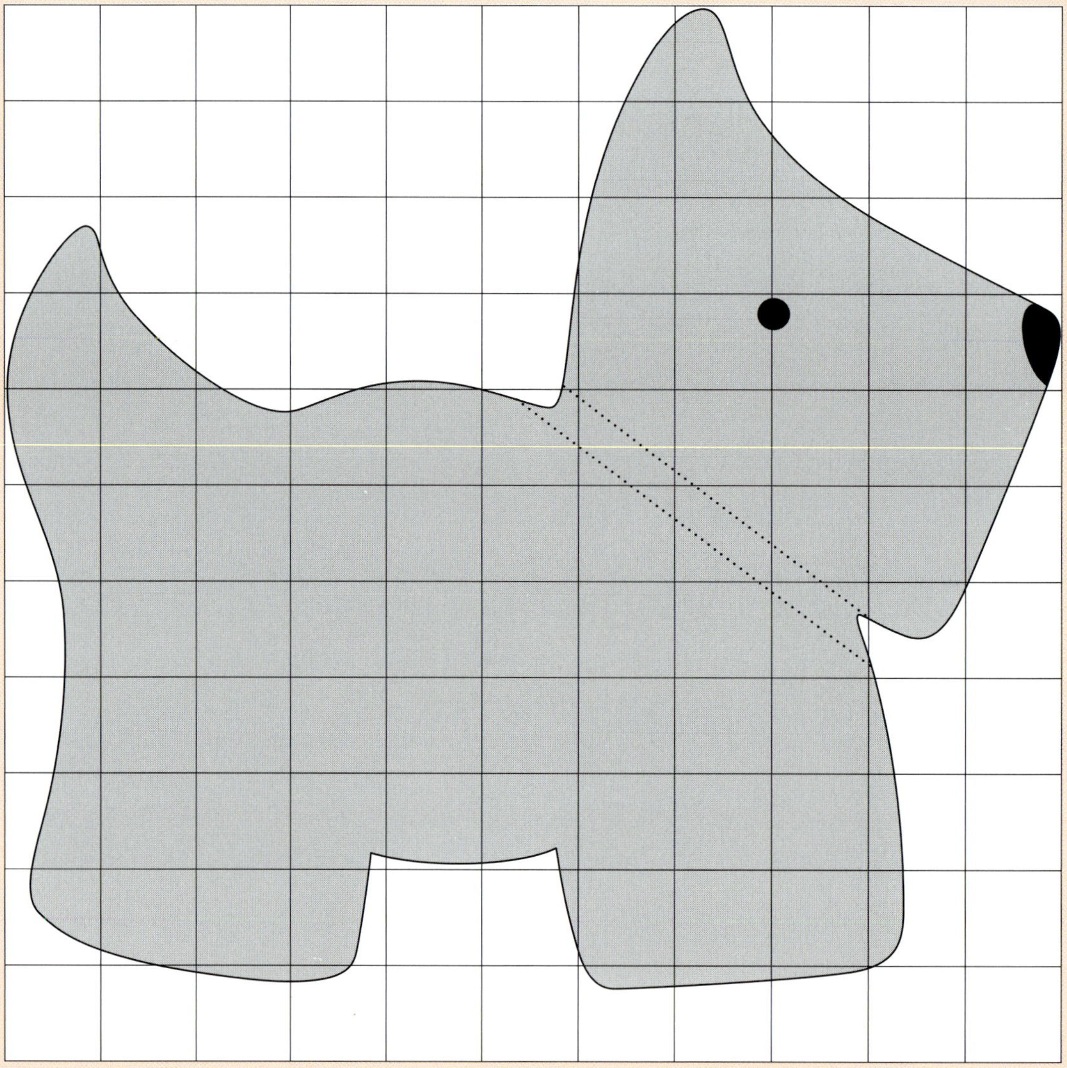

SCOTTY DOG PILLOW PATTERN

1 SQUARE = 1 INCH

dog front from the black check wool fabric. Cut the shape on the bias, allowing a ¼-inch seam. Cut out the dog back the same way only with red corduroy fabric on the straight grain.

2 Stitch piping around the outside edge of dog front. Stitch dog front to back with right sides facing, leaving an opening for turning. Trim and clip seam allowance. Turn to right side.

3 Stuff the shape with batting. Stitch the opening closed.

4 With two plies of black floss, outline-stitch (see *page 190*) the nose. Fill in with satin stitches.

5 Using the pattern as a guide, sew on white button eye with black floss through all layers. Add a French knot, *page 190,* to the center of the button.

6 Make a small bow at the center of the ribbon. Hand-stitch to center of collar. Sew dog button to the middle of the bow with red floss. Trim ribbon ends as necessary, turning under raw edge. Hand-stitch collar in place. Add jingle bells to collar as shown.

MANTEL MESSAGE

Chunky wood letters are painted then decoupaged to create a hopeful message Mary sends to everyone near and dear.

WHAT YOU'LL NEED

Tracing paper
Pencil
Seven 2-inch-thick pieces of pine, each approximately 9×9 inches
Saw
Sandpaper; tack cloth
White spray primer
Red acrylic or spray paint
White acrylic paint
Flat paintbrush
Wrapping papers, greeting cards, and decorative papers
Scissors
Paper punch
Decoupage medium
Fine liner paint brush
Black fine-point permanent marking pen

HERE'S HOW

1 Trace the patterns, *pages 154–155,* onto tracing paper. Cut out and trace onto wood. Cut out the letters with a saw.

2 Sand the edges, and wipe off dust with a tack cloth.

3 Prime letters with white spray primer. Let dry.

4 Paint the letters red using spray or acrylic paint. Let dry. Paint a second coat if needed. Let dry. Paint a ¼-inch white border around each letter. Let dry.

5 Gather papers for decoupaging onto letters. Cut out various motifs, such as flowers, toys, or packages. You can make your own gift packages to decoupage by cutting out various papers in squares and rectangles. Use a paper punch to cut out small dots for a garland.

6 To decoupage the cutouts onto the letters, paint decoupage medium onto the

(continued on page 154)

MANTEL MESSAGE *continued*

painted red surface. Position the cutouts, and paint decoupage medium over the papers as you work. When done, add details using paint and a marking pen. Paint ribbons on the packages using a liner brush. Use a fine-point, permanent black marker to outline the pieces. Let dry.

7 Coat the entire piece with another coat of decoupage medium. Let dry.

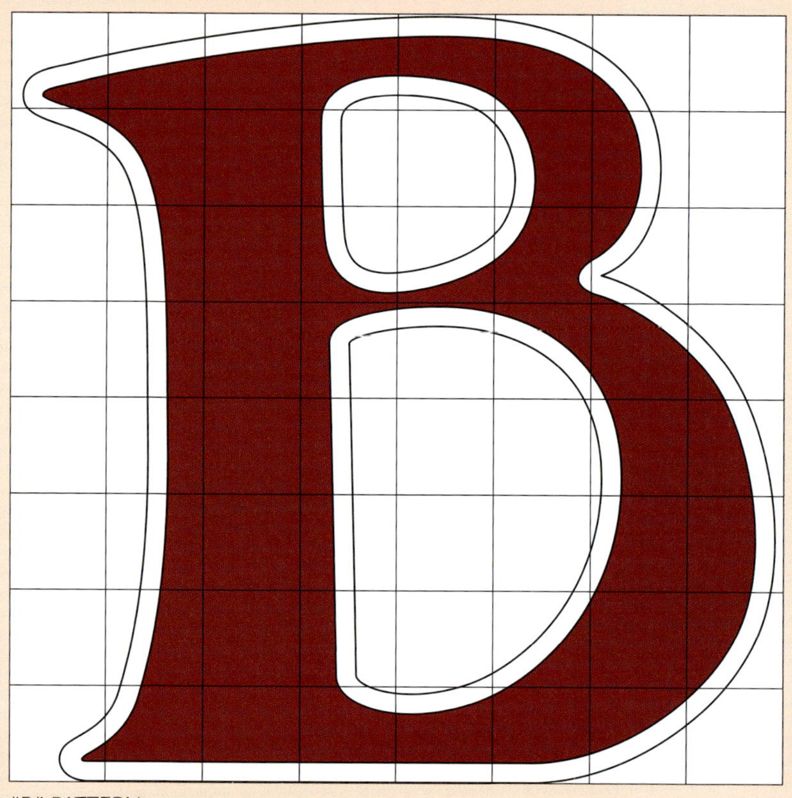

"B" PATTERN 1 SQUARE = 1 INCH

"L" PATTERN 1 SQUARE = 1 INCH

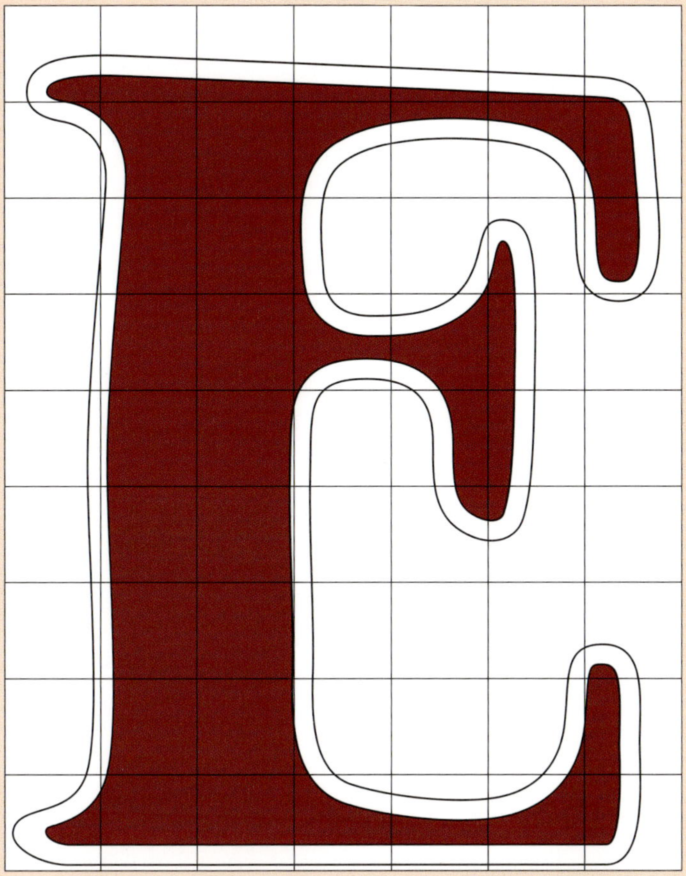

"E" PATTERN 1 SQUARE = 1 INCH

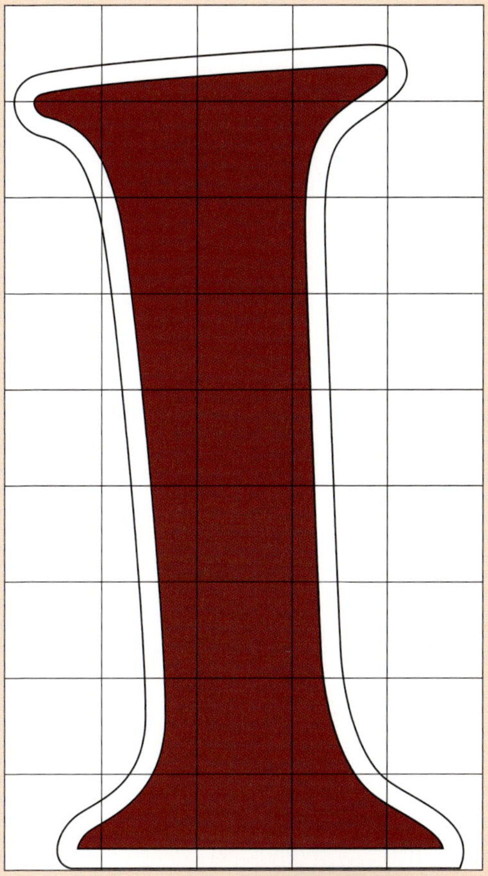

"I" PATTERN 1 SQUARE = 1 INCH

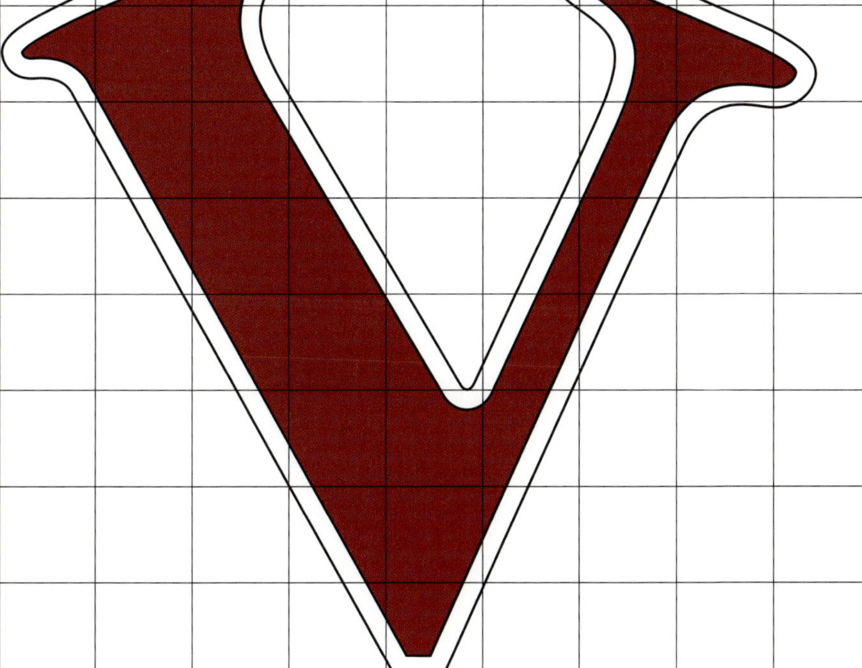

"V" PATTERN 1 SQUARE = 1 INCH

JESTER BEAR

Bears are one of Mary's favorite toys and this one exudes the warmth of Christmas.

WHAT YOU'LL NEED

for bear

1 yard of textured felt in light brown
Press cloth
6×12-inch piece of beige imitation suede
6×12-inch piece of lightweight fusible interfacing
Matching thread
Extra-strong tan button/carpet thread
Awl; poly-fil batting
Poly-fil pellets for stuffing bear
Eight 1¾-inch hardwood discs for arm and leg joints
Two 3-inch hardwood discs for head and neck joints
Five ½-inch and five 1-inch washers
Five 2½-inch cotter pins
1 yard of 2¼-inch-wide double-faced red satin ribbon
Two ⅝-inch brown eyes with shanks
#3 brown pearl cotton
#3 gray pearl cotton
Powder blush
1½-inch gold bell
Miniature Christmas ball and lightbulb
Long doll needle; T-pins

for hat

6×15-inch piece of green felt
6×15-inch piece of yellow felt
½ yard of decorative rickrack
50–60 red 5mm pom-poms
Fabric glue

HERE'S HOW

1 A ¼-inch seam allowance is included in each pattern piece. Stitch the seams with right sides facing. Cut out pieces according to the full-size patterns, *pages 158–163*. For bear body, lay out pattern pieces on wrong side of fabric, and trace around each piece. Remember to reverse pattern pieces where necessary. Transfer all joint and opening placements to fabrics.

2 Using a press cloth, press interfacing to wrong side of suede. Trace and cut out paw and foot pad pattern pieces.

3 Sew body front seam. Sew body back seam, leaving an opening for turning. Sew front to back at body side seams, leaving neck edge open. Turn to right side. Turn neck edge under ¼ inch. With button/carpet thread, gather neck tightly. Secure thread ends.

4 Sew arm pieces together in pairs. Sew paw pad to inner arm. Sew outer arm to inner arm, leaving an opening for turning. Turn to right side.

5 Sew legs together in pairs, leaving an opening for turning. Say-stitch around bottom of leg ¼ inch from edge. Baste foot pad to bottom edge of leg, matching center front and center back seam. Stitch and turn to right side.

6 With an awl, make a hole in arms, legs, and body at marked joints. Assemble bear in this manner through openings in arm and leg pieces: Push cotter pin with small washer and disc through hole in each arm, and through joint hole in body. Place disc and large washer on the cotter pin inside body. Separate and bend ends of cotter pin to washer to tightly hold arms and body together. Repeat for legs.

7 Sew dart in side head pieces. Sew side head pieces and head top together from tip of gusset to side head piece from tip of nose to back of the neck, easing pieces together to fit. Repeat for other side. Leave neck open.

8 Stay-stitch around neck ¼ inch from edge. Clip curves as necessary. Turn to right side. Stuff head firmly with poly-fil.

9 Place small washer on cotter pin, then disc, and insert into neck opening of head. At neck edge, turn neck under ¼ inch. With button/carpet thread, gather neck opening tightly over disc with cotter pin extended. Secure thread ends. Join head to body by pushing extended cotter pins through the body. Place disc and large washer on cotter pin inside the body. Separate and bend ends of

[continued on page 158]

JESTER BEAR *continued*

cotter pin to washer to tightly secure head to body. Stuff feet and paws with poly-fil. Stuff remaining part of legs and arms with pellets. Stitch openings of arms and legs closed.

10 Sew ears together in pairs, leaving bottom edge open. Turn under ¼ inch at bottom edge of ear, and slip-stitch closed. Pin ears to head with T-pins, and sew in place with button/carpet thread and a long doll needle. Pass needle through head from back to front and back through the ears.

11 With awl, make a hole in the head for eye placement. Thread shank of eye with two strands each of a 30-inch length of button/carpet thread. Tie threads around shank at center of threads. Thread long doll needle with two threads. Push the needle through the eye hole and out behind the ear. Repeat with other two threads coming out ⅛-inch from first stitch. Knot the thread ends, pulling eye into place. Secure thread ends invisibly behind ear. Clip thread. Repeat for second eye.

12 For nose, satin-stitch (see *page 190*) a triangle shape with brown pearl cotton. Add pearl cotton mouth using the photo, *page 157*, as a guide. Outline stitch two rows with gray for eyebrows. Brush blush on ears, cheeks, and nose.

13 Tie ribbon into bow around neck with bell, Christmas ball, and lightbulb trim.

14 For hat, cut pattern pieces from yellow and green felt. Stitch short end of hatband with ¼-inch seam. Turn right side out. Stitch two opposite crown sections from band to top point of crown, indicated by a dot on pattern. Refold crown, and stitch continuously the remaining crown sections from band, across top point to opposite side of band. Turn hat to right side. Sew a ¼ inch ease stitch on straight edge of yellow jester point felt piece. Top stitch jester point piece to hat 1 inch from edge of band. Top stitch rickrack along right side edge of band. Turn band up over topstitching of jester point piece. Glue pom-poms on points.

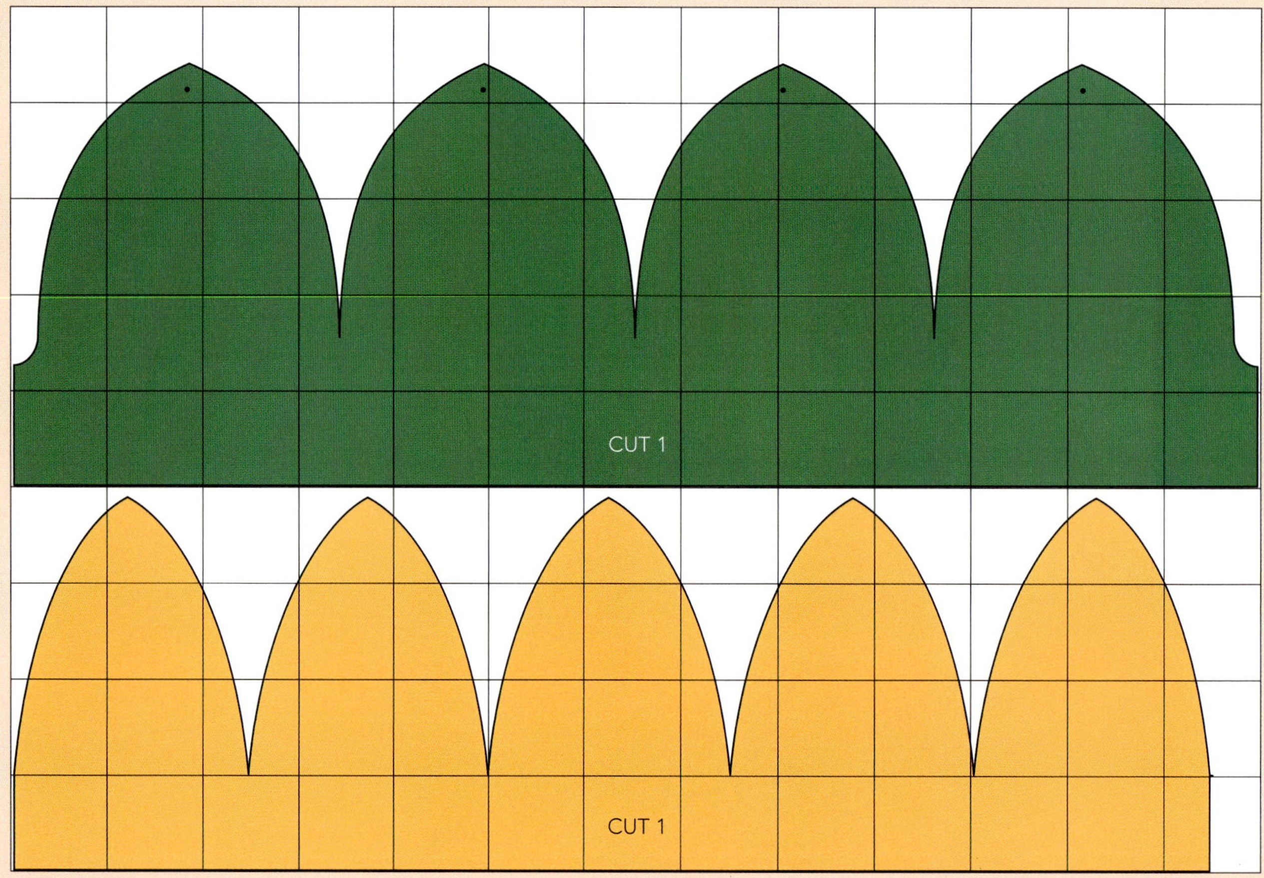

JESTER BEAR HAT PATTERNS

1 SQUARE = 1 INCH

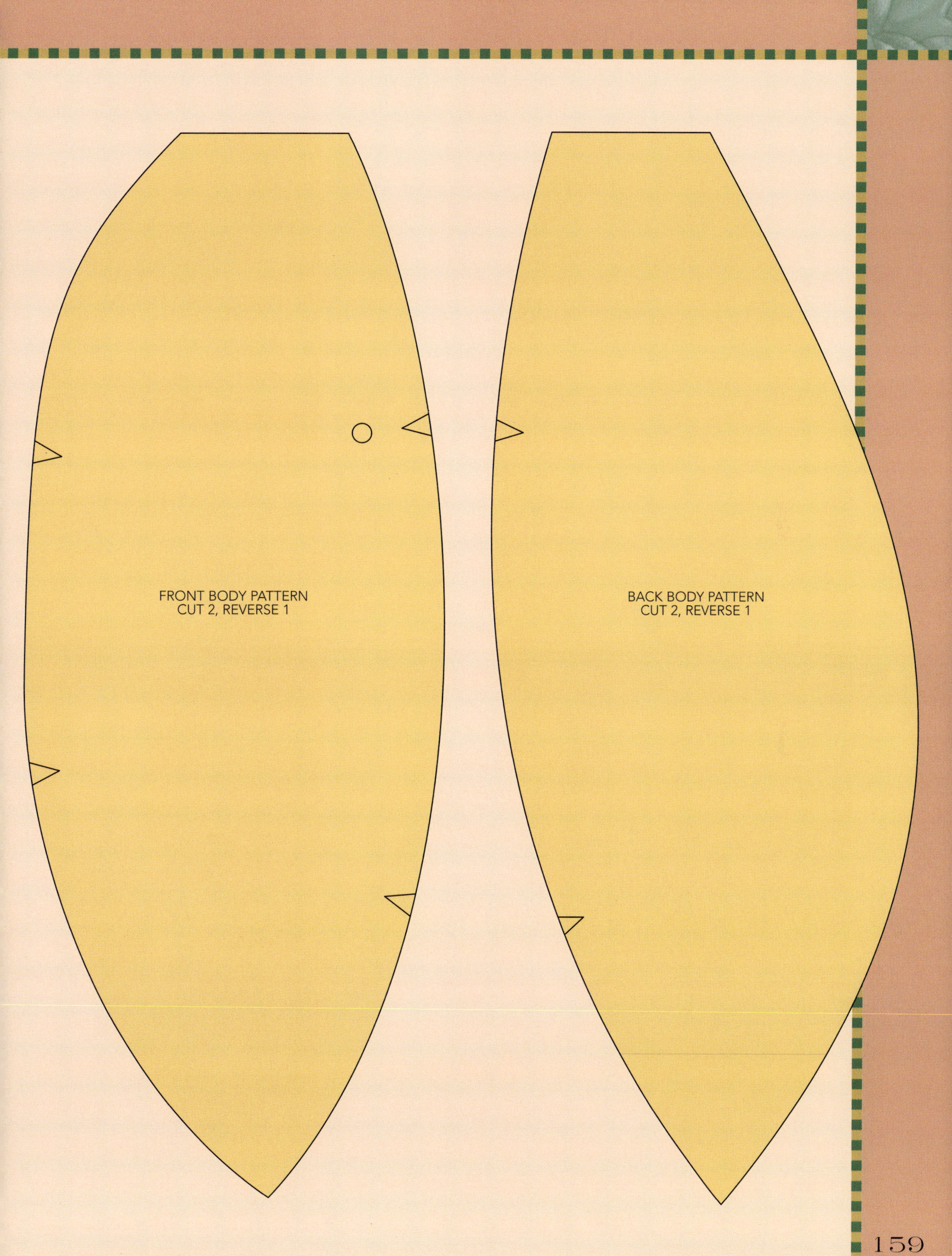
FRONT BODY PATTERN
CUT 2, REVERSE 1
BACK BODY PATTERN
CUT 2, REVERSE 1

JESTER BEAR *continued*

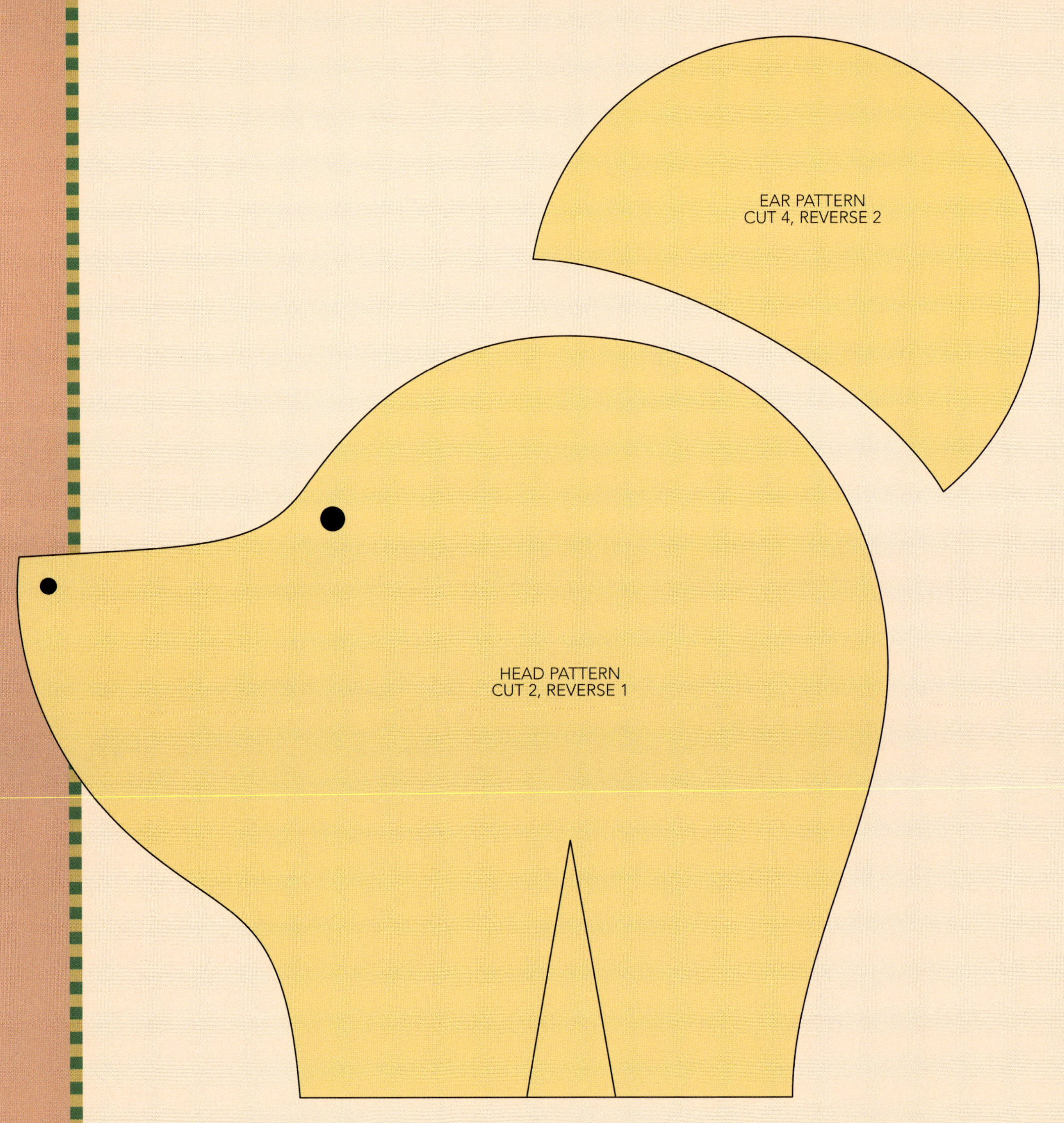

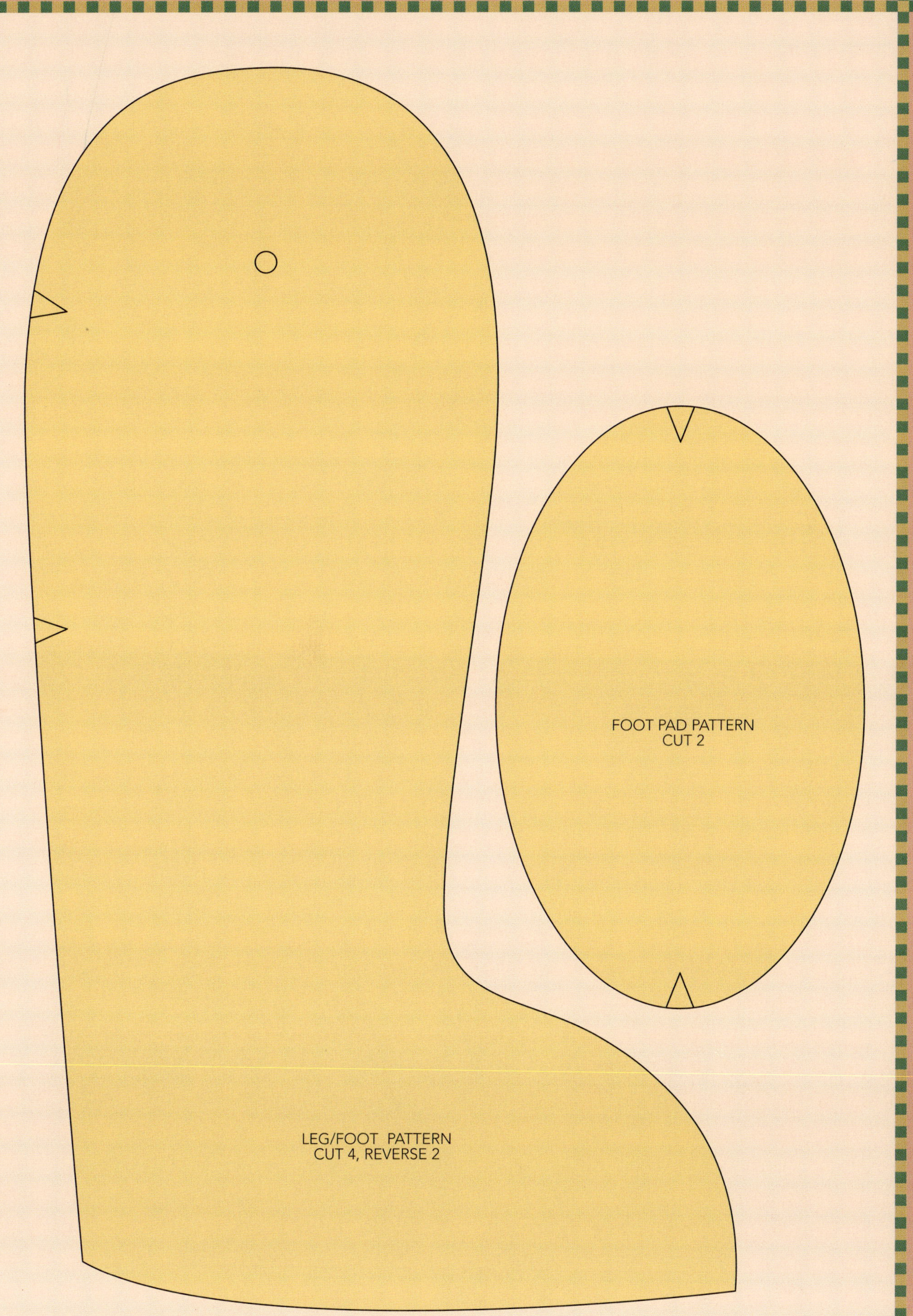
FOOT PAD PATTERN
CUT 2
LEG/FOOT PATTERN
CUT 4, REVERSE 2

JESTER BEAR *continued*

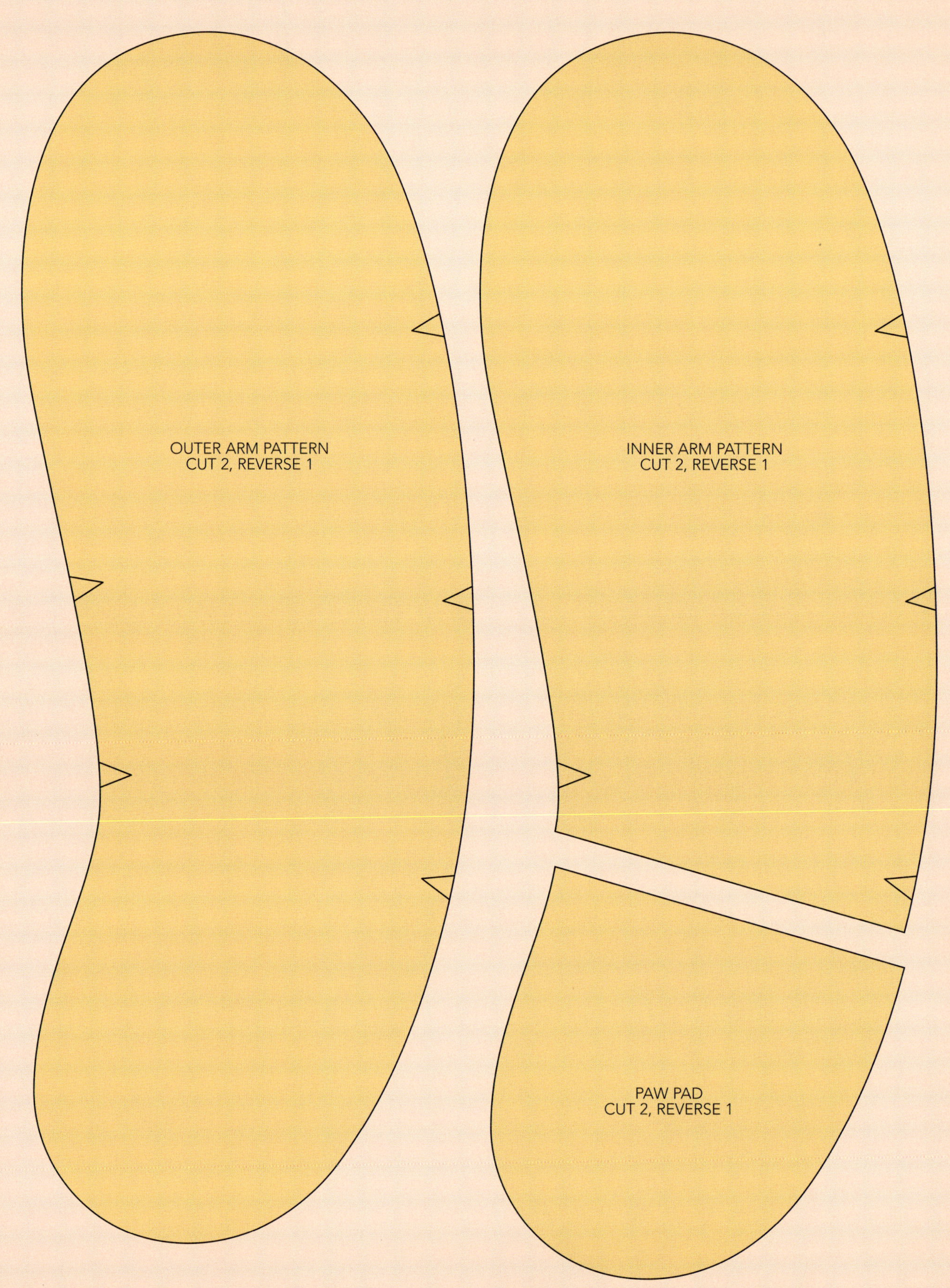

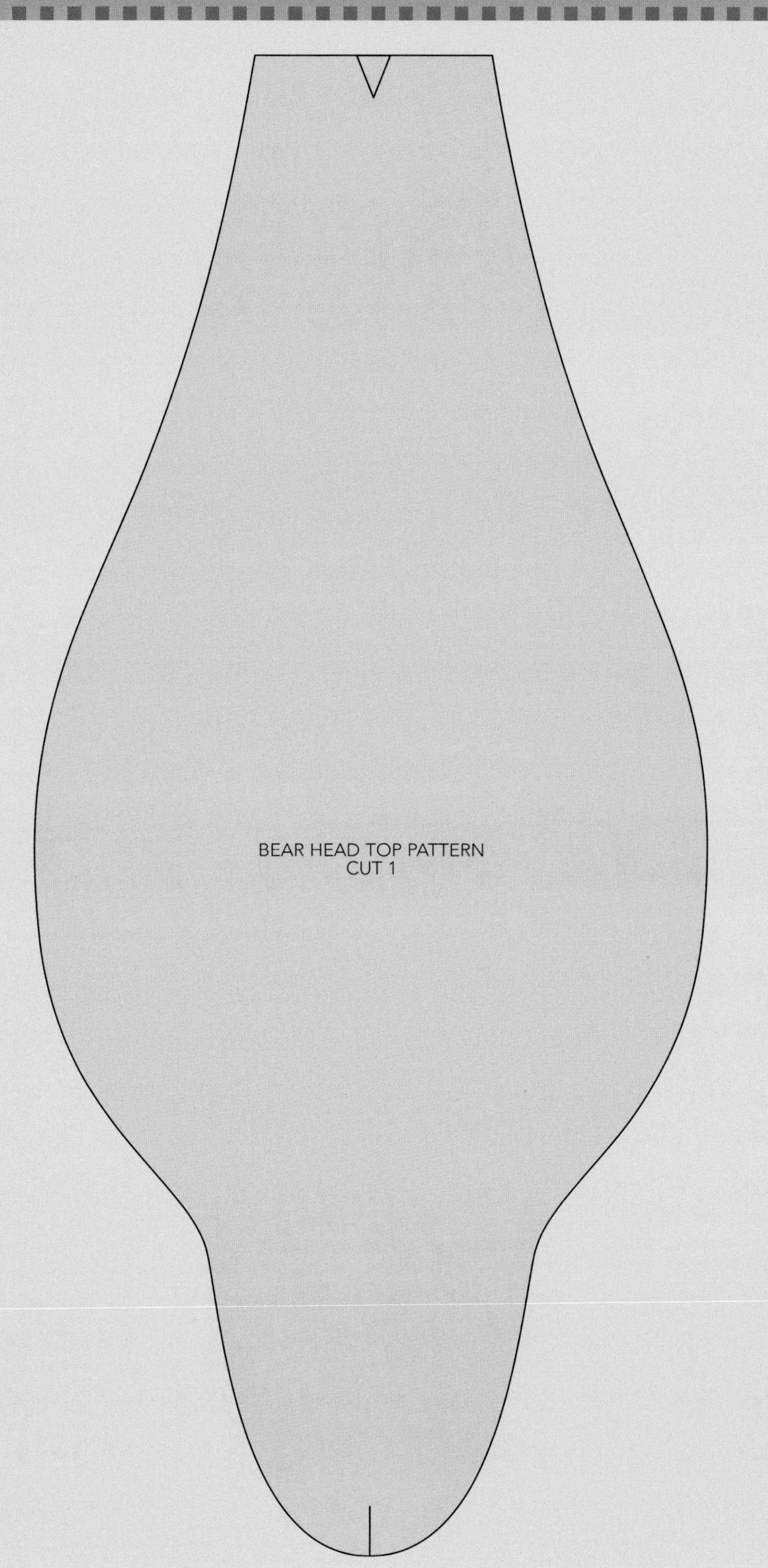
BEAR HEAD TOP PATTERN
CUT 1

CUDDLE-TIME DOLL

Made from pastel, soft-as-a-kitten yarns, this precious crocheted doll is just like the one on Mary's card. The braided belt, stitched facial details, and button accents add charm to this happy and cuddly friend.

WHAT YOU'LL NEED

Caron Simply Soft yarn in 9716 goldenrod (gold)
Caron Wintuk yarns in 3025 baby pink (pink) and 3256 jonquil (yellow)
Red Heart Soft yarn in 7672 light yellow-green (green)
Cotton embroidery floss in DMC 321 red, 3021 brown, and 3689 pink
Size E/4 aluminum crochet hook
Two ⅞-inch-diameter wood buttons
Red acrylic paint
Polyester stuffing
Crewel needle

HERE'S HOW

Note: *Gauge: 5 sts = 1 inch, 5 rnds = 1 inch*

for hat

Rnd 1: Beg at top, with yellow, ch 2, work 6 sc in 2nd ch from hk. Do not join rnds, mark beg of each rnd with a strand of contrasting yarn.

Rnd 2: * Sc in sc, (2 sc in next sc = inc made), sc in rem 4 sc (7sc).

Rnd 3: Sc in each st around (7sc).

Rnd 4: * Sc in next 2 sc, 1 inc in next st rep from * once, sc in last st (9 sc).

Rnd 5: Sc in each st around (9 sc).

Rnd 6: * Sc in next 2 sc, 1 inc in next st; rep from * twice (12 sc).

Rnd 7: Sc in each st around (12 sc).

Rnd 8: * Sc in each of next 3 sc, 1 inc in next st; rep from * twice (15 sc).

Rnds 9 & 10: Sc in each st around (15 sc).

Rnd 11: * Sc in each of next 4 sc, 1 inc in next st; rep from * twice (18 sc).

Rnds 12 & 13: Sc in each st around (18).

Rnd 14: * Sc in each of 5 sc, 1 inc in next st; rep from * twice (21 sc).

Rnds 15 & 16: Sc in each st around (21 sc).

Rnd 17: * Sc in each of 6 sc, 1 inc in next st; rep from * twice (24 sc).

Rnds 18 & 19: Sc in each st around (24 sc).

(continued on page 166)

CUDDLE-TIME DOLL *continued*

Rnd 20: * Sc in each of 7 sc, 1 inc in next st; rep from * twice (27 sc).
Rnds 21 & 22: Sc in each st around (27 sc).
Rnd 23: * Sc in each of 8 sc, 1 inc in next st; rep from * twice (30 sc).
Rnd 24: Sc in each st around (30 sc).
Rnd 25: * Sc in each of 9 sc, 1 inc in next st; rep from * twice (33 sc).
Rnds 26 & 27: Sc in each st around (33 sc).
Rnd 28: * Sc in each of 10 sc, 1 inc in next st; rep from * twice (36 sc).
Rnds 29–31: Sc in each st around (36 sc), fasten off yellow.
Rnd 32: With wrong side of hat facing (inside area) attach green in first sc with sl st. Sc in same st and in each sc around (36 sc).
Rnd 33: * Sc in each of 8 sc, 1 inc in next st, rep from * 3 times (40 sc).
Rnd 34: Using back lps only, * sc in each of 7 sc; 1 inc in next st, rep from * 4 times (45 sc).
Rnds 35–40: Sc in each st around (45 sc).
Rnd 41: Sl st in each st around. Fasten off. Turn up green area to form cuff on hat. Attach green to front lps of rnd 34, sl st in each lp around. Fasten off.

for head

Rnd 1: Beg at top of head with pink, ch 2 work 6 sc in 2nd ch from hk (6 sc).
Rnd 2: Work 1 inc in each st around (12 sc).
Rnd 3: * Sc in next 2 sts, 1 inc in next st; rep from * 3 times (16 sc).
Rnd 4: * Sc in each of 3 sc, 1 inc in next st, rep from * 3 times (20 sc).
Rnd 5: Sc in each of 4 sc *, * 1 inc in next st, sc in next st, 1 inc in next st *, sc in each of 7 sc, rep bet *s once, sc in each of 3 rem sc (24 sc).
Rnd 6: Sc in each st around (24 sc).
Rnd 7: Sc in each of 5 sc, * 1 inc in next st, sc in next st, 1 inc in next st *, sc in each of 9 sc, rep bet *s once, sc in each of 4 rem sc (28 sc).
Rnd 8: Sc in each of 4 sc *, 1 inc in next st, sc in each of 4 sts, 1 inc in next st *, sc in each of 9 sc, rep bet *s once, sc in each of 3 rem sc (32 sc).
Rnd 9: Sc in each st around (32 sc).
Rnd 10: Sc in each of 6 sc, * 1 inc in next st, sc in each of 2 sc, 1 inc in next st * sc in each of 13 sc, rep bet *s once, sc in each of 5 rem sc (36 sc).
Rnds 11–17: Sc in each st around (36 sc).
Rnd 18: Sc in each of 11 sc, mark next st, sc in each of 17 sc, mark next st, sc in each of 8 rem sc (36 sc).
Rnd 19: Sc in each of 11 sc, (2 sc tog—dec over 2 sts made); * sc in each of 4 sc, dec over next 2 sc; rep from * twice, sc in each of 5 rem sc (32 sc).
Rnd 20: Sc in each of 8 sc, dec over next 2 sc, * sc in each of 3 sc, dec over next 2 sc; rep from * 3 times, sc in each of 2 rem sc (27 sc).
Rnd 21: Sc in each st around (27 sc).
Rnd 22: Sc in each of 7 sc, * dec over next 2 sc, sc in each of 4 sc * rep bet *s twice, sc in each of 2 rem sc (24 sc).
Rnds 23 & 24: Sc in each st around (24 sts) fasten off pink. Stuff the head, pushing extra stuffing near marks in rnd 18 for cheeks and toward dec area to shape chin. The head shaping should look flattened, not rounded.

for body

Rnd 25: Count over 3 sts (include first st of last rnd) attach green in next st, sc in same st and in each of next 6 sc, * 1 inc in next st, sc in next st, 1 inc in next st *, sc in each of 8 sc, rep bet *s once, sc in each of 4 rem sc (28 sc). (Inc areas are shoulders.)
Rnd 26: Sc in each of 8 sc, 1 inc in next st, sc in each of 12 sc, 1 inc in next st, sc in each of 6 rem sc (30 sc). Mark each inc of this rnd for attachment of arms.
Rnd 27: Sc in each of 6 sc, 1 inc in next st, sc in each of 18 sc, 1 inc in next st, sc in each of 4 rem sc (32 sc).
Rnd 28: Sc in each of 10 sc. 1 inc in next st, sc in each of 13 sc, 1 inc in next st, sc in each of 7 rem sc (34 sc).
Rnd 29: Sc in each of 9 sc, * 1 inc in next st, sc in next st, 1 inc in next st *, sc in each of 13 sc, rep bet *s, sc in each of 6 rem sc (38 sc).
Rnd 30: Sc in each st around (38 sc).
Rnd 31: * Sc in each of 8 sc, 1 inc in next st; rep from * 3 times, sc in each of 2 rem sc (42 sc).
Rnd 32 & 33: Sc in each st around (42 sc).
Rnd 34: Sc in each of 14 sc, 1 inc in next st, sc in each of 17 sc, 1 inc in next st, sc in each of 9 rem sc (44 sc).
Rnd 35: Sc in each st around (44 sc).
Rnd 36: Sc in each of 13 sc, * 1 inc in next st, sc in each of 2 sc, 1 inc in next st *, sc in each of 15 sc, rep bet *s once, sc in each of 8 rem sc (48 sc).

Rnds 37 & 38: Sc in each st around (48 sc).
Rnd 39: Sc in each of 14 sc, * 1 inc in next st, sc in each of 3 sc, 1 inc in next st *, sc in each of 16 sc, rep bet *'s once, sc in each of 8 rem sts (52 sc).
Rnds 40 & 41: Sc in each st around (52 sc).
Rnd 42: Sc in each of 14 sc, * 1 inc in next st, sc in each of 5 sc, 1 inc in next st *, sc in each of 19 sc, rep bet *'s once, sc in each of 5 rem sc (56 sc).
Rnds 43 & 44: Sc in each st around (56 sc).

for first leg

Rnd 1: Sc in each of 5 sc, sl st into next st, ch 8, skip next 27 sts, sl st in next st. (Leg openings formed.) Ch 1, turn, * sc in each of 8 ch and continue around working 1 sc in each of 27 sc – 35 sc.
Rnd 2: * Sc in next sc, dec over next 2 sc; rep from * twice, sc in each of 11 sc, 1 inc in next st, sc in each of 3 sc, 1 inc in next st, sc in 10 rem sc (34 sc).
Rnds 3–12: Sc in each st around (34 sc).
Rnd 13: * Sc in each of 6 sc, dec over next 2 sc; rep from * 3 times, sc in each of 2 rem sc (30 sc).
Rnd 14: Using front lps only, sc in each sc around (30 sc).
Rnd 15: Sc in each st around (30 sc).
Rnd 16: Sl st in each st around (30 sl st). Fasten off.

for second leg

Working along opposite edge of the ch 8, join yarn in first rem ch. Ch 1, sc in same ch and next 7 ch; sc in each of next 27 sc – 35 sts. Rep Rnds 2–16 as for First Leg. Stuff body and upper legs.

for shoes

Rnd 1: Turn back leg rnds 14–16. Attach gold yarn at center back of 13, sc in each lp around (30 sc).
Rnd 2: Mark 3 sc on front of 1. Sc in each sc around, working 1 inc in each of 3 marked sc on front, sc in each of rem sc (33 sc).
Rnd 3: Sc in each sc to 3-inc-group. *1 inc in next st, sc in next st; rep from * twice, sc in each of rem sc (36 sc).
Rnd 4: Sc in each sc to sc before first inc of rnd 3, 1 inc in next st, sc in each of 7 sc, 1 inc in next st, sc in each rem sc (38 sc).
Rnd 5: Sc in each st around (38 sc).
Rnd 6: Sc in 1 inc in next st, sc in each of 3 sts, 1 inc in next st, sc in each rem sc (40 sc).
Rnds 7 & 8: Sc in each st around (40 sc).
Rnd 9: (Ridge stitch) Sl st around each sc.
Rnd 10: Using back lps only on sc of 8, * sc in each of 3 sc, dec over next 2 sc; rep from * 7 times (32 sc).
Rnd 11: Sc in 6 sc; x sc 2 tog, sc in 4 sc; rep from * 3 times, sc in last 2 sc (28 sc).
Rnd 12: Dec over next 2 sc, sc in next sc, rep from * 7 times, sc in 4 rem sc (20 sc). Fasten off. Complete stuffing lower leg and shoe. Sew base of shoe closed lengthwise.

for shoe sole

Rnd 1: With gold, ch 6, sc in 2nd ch from hk and in each of 3 ch, work 3 sc in last ch, continue across opposite side of ch, sc in each of 3 lps, 2 sc in last lp (12 sc).
Rnd 2: 1 inc in next sc, sc in each of 3 sc, 1 inc in each of next 3 sc, sc in each of 3 sc, 1

(continued on page 168)

CUDDLE-TIME DOLL *continued*

inc in each of 2 rem sc (18 sc).
Rnd 3: * inc in each of next 2 sc, sc in 3 sc * rep bet x's 3 times; inc in each of next 2 sts, sc in rem sc.
Rnd 4: * 1 inc in next sc, sc in next sc *, 1 inc in next sc, sc in each of 5 sc, rep bet *s 4 times, 1 inc in next st, sc in each of 5 sc, rep bet *s twice (35 sc).
Rnd 5: Sc in each of 2 sc , * 1 inc in next st, sc in each of 10 sc, 1 inc in next st *, sc in each of 2 sc, 1 inc in next st, sc in each of 2 sc, rep bet *s once, sc in each of 4 sc (40 sc). Fasten off.
Line up shoe sole with base of shoe. Pin in place, sl st together using black lps of ridge stitch and back lps on sc of sole.

for collar

Rnd 1: With yellow, ch 27, sc in 2nd ch from hk and in each of next 24 ch. Work 4 sc in last ch. Continue across opposite side of ch, sc in each lp, work 3 sc in last lp.
Rnd 2: Sc in first sc and in each of next 25 sc, ch 1, sl st in each of next 2 sc, ch 1, sc in next sc and in each of 25 sts, ch 1, sl st in each of next 2 sts, ch 1. Do not turn.
Rnd 3: Sc in first sc and in each of next 25 sc. Fasten off. Fold collar to form a log shape. Whipstitch sides tog. Fit around neck with the edges meeting at back. Stitch edges tog. Tack in place.

for arms

Rnd 1: With gold yarn, ch 2, 6 sc in 2nd ch from hk (6 sc).
Rnd 2: * Sc in next st, 1 inc in next st; rep from * twice (9 sc).
Rnd 3: * Sc in each of 2 sc, 1 inc in next st; rep from * twice (12 sc).
Rnd 4: Sc in each st around (12 sc). Fasten off.
Rnd 5: Attach yellow, * sc in each of 3 sc, 1 inc in next st; rep from * twice (15 sc).
Rnd 6: Sc in each st around (15 sc).
Rnd 7: * Sc in each of 4 sc, 1 inc in next st, rep from * twice (18 sc), fasten off.
Rnds 8–10: Attach gold yarn, sc in each st around (18 sc) at end of 10, fasten off.
Rnds 11 & 12: Attach yellow, sc in each st around (18 sc).
Rnd 13: Using front lps only, * sc in each of 8 sc, 1 inc in next st; rep from * once (20 sc).
Rnd 14: Using back lps only, sl st in each st around, fasten off.

for hand

Turn back 13, 1: Attach pink to back lps of rnd 12, sc in each lp around (18 sc).
Rnds 15–18: Sc in each sc around (18 sc).
Rnd 19: * Sc in each of 2 sc, dec over next 2 sc; rep from * 3 times, sc in each of 2 rem sc (14 sc).
Rnd 20: * Sc in next st, dec over next 2 sc; rep from * 3 times, sc in each of 2 rem sc (10 sc), leaving an 8-inch tail, fasten off. Stuff arm. Thread tail into needle and back through rem 10 sts. Pull tightly to close opening. Attach arms to body by pinning in place on each side of body at markers. Tack in place with gold yarn.

for ears

Rnd 1: With pink, ch 2, 6 sc in 2nd ch from hk (6 sc).
Rnd 2: *1 inc in next st, sc in each of 2 sc; rep from * once (8 sc).
Rnd 3: Sc in next st, 1 inc in next st, sc in each of 3 sc, 1 inc in next st, sc in each of 2 rem sc (10 sc).
Rnd 4: Sc in each st around (10 sc). Fasten off.
Sew ears on each side of head bet rnds 14–18.

for features

Follow chart and instructions for placement.

for waistband

Using 8 strands of green, make a ch to fit around doll's waist. Tuck in ends at back and tack in place with green yarn.

for buttons

Paint wood buttons with red acrylic paint. Allow to dry. Sew in place with gold yarn.

for hat pom-pom

Using a 2-inch-wide piece of cardboard, place a 10-inch strand of gold yarn across cardboard. Wrap yarn around cardboard 100 times. Tie the 10-inch-long strand into a knot around center of yarn. Cut yarn ends, and trim to measure 1½ inches across. Sew to end of hat. Place hat on head, positioning cuff at back lower than front. Front cuff should be tacked in place ¼ inch above the eyes.

Note: The crochet abbreviations are on *page 191*.

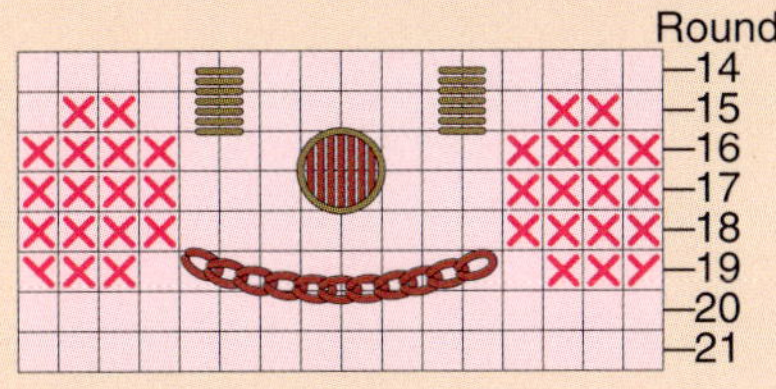

1 Square = 1 Stitch on face

Cuddle-Time Doll Face Key

Cross-Stitch

✕ Cheek – DMC 3689 Pink (3X)

Padded Satin Stitch

— Eyes – DMC 3021 Brown (6X)

| Nose – DMC 321 Red (6X)

Stem Stitch

○ Nose – DMC 3021 Brown (3X)

Chain Stitch

⬭ Mouth – DMC 321 Red (3X)

CHAIN STITCH

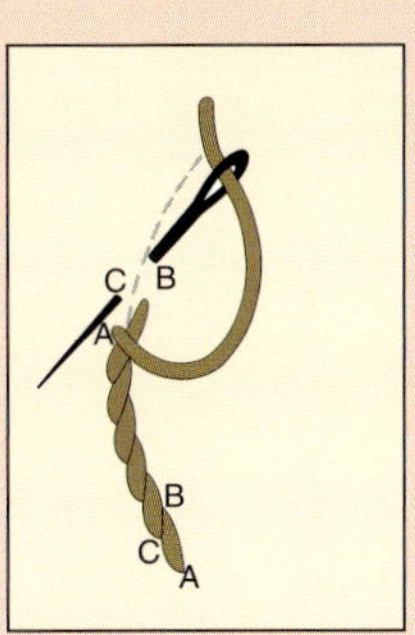

STEM STITCH

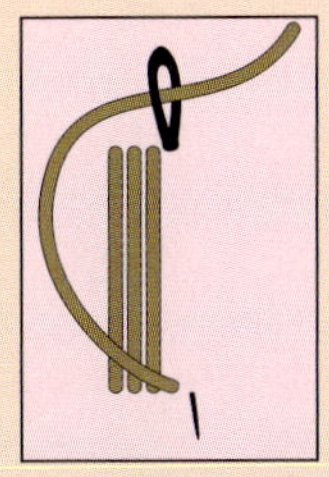

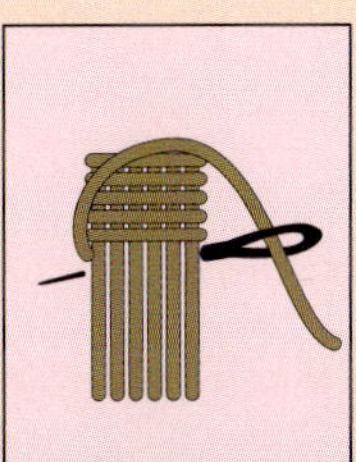

Step 1

Step 2

PADDED SATIN STITCH

FAMILY OF FOUR ORNAMENTS

These charming characters, resembling a collection of Mary's stacking toys, will add whimsy to your Christmas tree or holiday greenery. Turn the page for charts and instructions.

Christmas Tea for all the Toys

FAMILY OF FOUR ORNAMENTS *continued*

WHAT YOU'LL NEED

- One sheet of 14-count plastic canvas
- Scissors
- Cotton embroidery floss as listed in key; needle
- 6×5-inch piece of blue imitation suede for dad
- 6×4-inch piece of gold imitation suede for mom
- 6×4-inch piece of red imitation suede for boy
- 4×4-inch piece of pink imitation suede for girl
- Two coordinating colors of floss from each design
- Fabric glue
- Pinking shears
- 8 gold star pony beads

HERE'S HOW

1 Cut the sheet of plastic canvas into quarters. Find the center of the desired chart, *below and opposite,* and the center of one piece of plastic; begin stitching there. Use two plies of floss to work the cross-stitches over one square of plastic. Work French knots, *page 190,* using two plies.

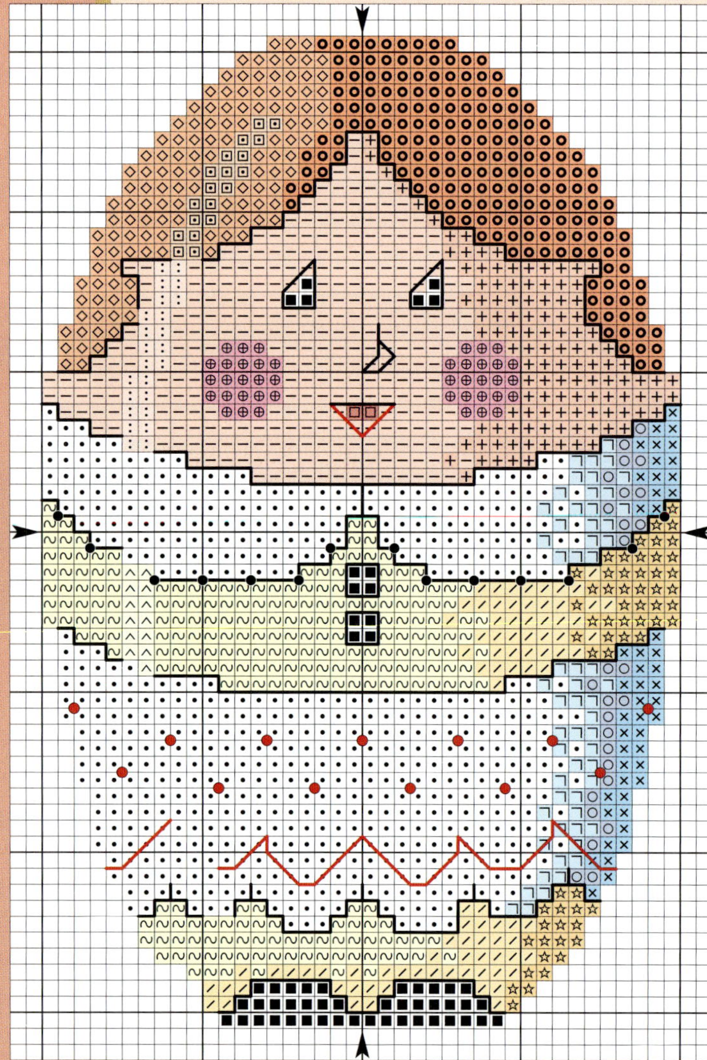

MOM CHART

Anchor	DMC
002	000 White
1006	304 Christmas red
403	310 Black
1038	519 Sky blue

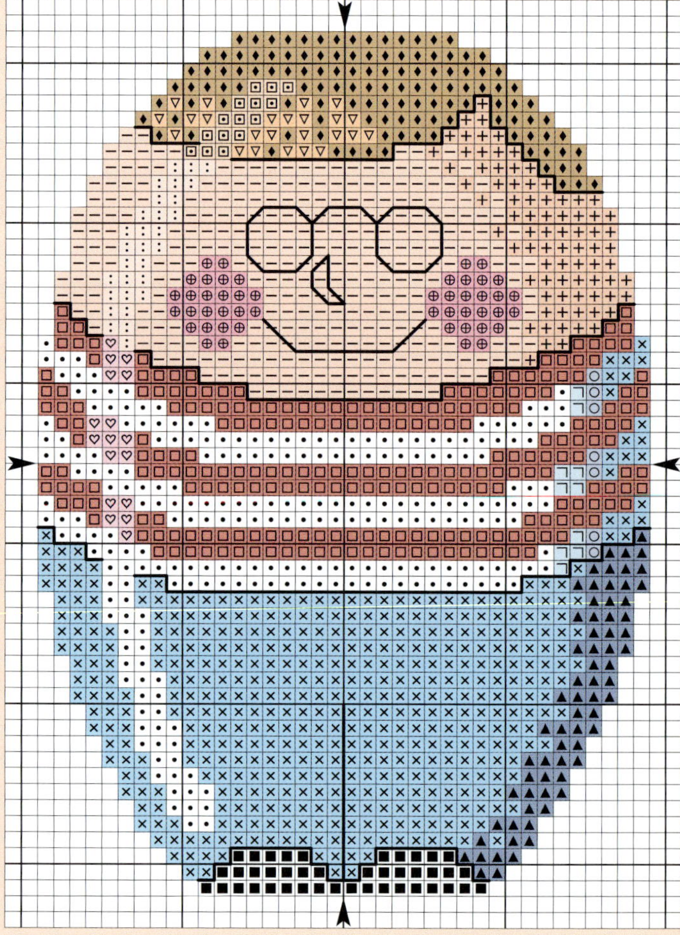

BOY CHART

Anchor	DMC	Anchor	DMC
305	725 True topaz	075	962 Medium rose-pink
293	727 Pale topaz	433	996 Electric blue
868	754 Medium peach	292	3078 Lemon
339	920 Medium copper	025	3716 Light rose-pink
337	922 Light copper	1031	3753 Antique blue
882	945 Dark ivory	169	3765 Peacock blue
1012	948 Light peach	1048	3826 Golden brown
1010	951 Medium ivory	313	3854 Autumn gold

Work the other stitches as indicated in key.

2 Carefully trim around each stitched design, one square beyond stitching.

3 Center and glue the stitched pieces onto corresponding colors of suede. Trim close to design edge with pinking shears.

4 For each design, cut 1 yard each of two coordinating strands of floss. Twist together until strands start to kink back on themselves. Fold strands in half allowing cording to twist again making a 4-ply cord.

5 Glue cord trim along the edge of the design, matching the center of the cord to the center bottom of the design. Allow long tails at the center top of the head. With a few whipstitches of thread, secure the cording at the center top of the head

6 Tie a knot close to the end of the tails. For each tail, slip on a star bead, and tie another knot. Trim the ends close to the knot. Add glue to the cord inside of the bead to secure.

Dad stitch count: *71 high x 46 wide*

Dad finished design sizes:
14-count fabric – 5 x 3¼ inches
16-count fabric – 4½ x 2⅞ inches
18-count fabric – 4 x 2½ inches

Mom stitch count: *62 high x 40 wide*

Mom finished design sizes:
14-count fabric – 4½ x 2⅞ inches
16-count fabric – 3⅞ x 2½ inches
18-count fabric – 3½ x 2¼ inches

Boy stitch count: *54 high x 38 wide*

Boy finished design sizes:
14-count fabric – 3⅞ x 2¾ inches
16-count fabric – 3⅜ x 2⅜ inches
18-count fabric – 3 x 2⅛ inches

Girl stitch count: *40 high x 28 wide*

Girl finished design sizes:
14-count fabric – 2⅞ x 2 inches
16-count fabric – 2½ x 1¾ inches
18-count fabric – 2¼ x 1½ inches

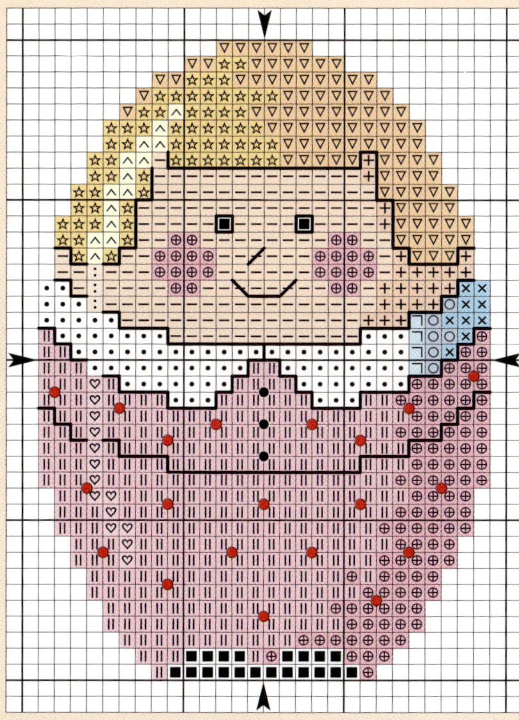

GIRL CHART

BLENDED NEEDLE

002 / 1012 — 000 White (1X) and 948 Light peach (1X)

002 / 1010 — 000 White (1X) and 951 Medium ivory (1X)

002 / 292 — 000 White (1X) and 3078 Lemon (1X)

002 / 025 — 000 White (1X) and 3716 Light rose-pink (1X)

BACKSTITCH

1006 — 304 Christmas red – mom's dress (1X) and mom's mouth (2X)

403 — 310 Black – all remaining stitches (1X)

FRENCH KNOT

002 — 000 White – dad's eye highlights

1006 — 304 Christmas red – girl's dress and mom's dress

403 — 310 Black – dad's mouth, girl's dress and mom's collar

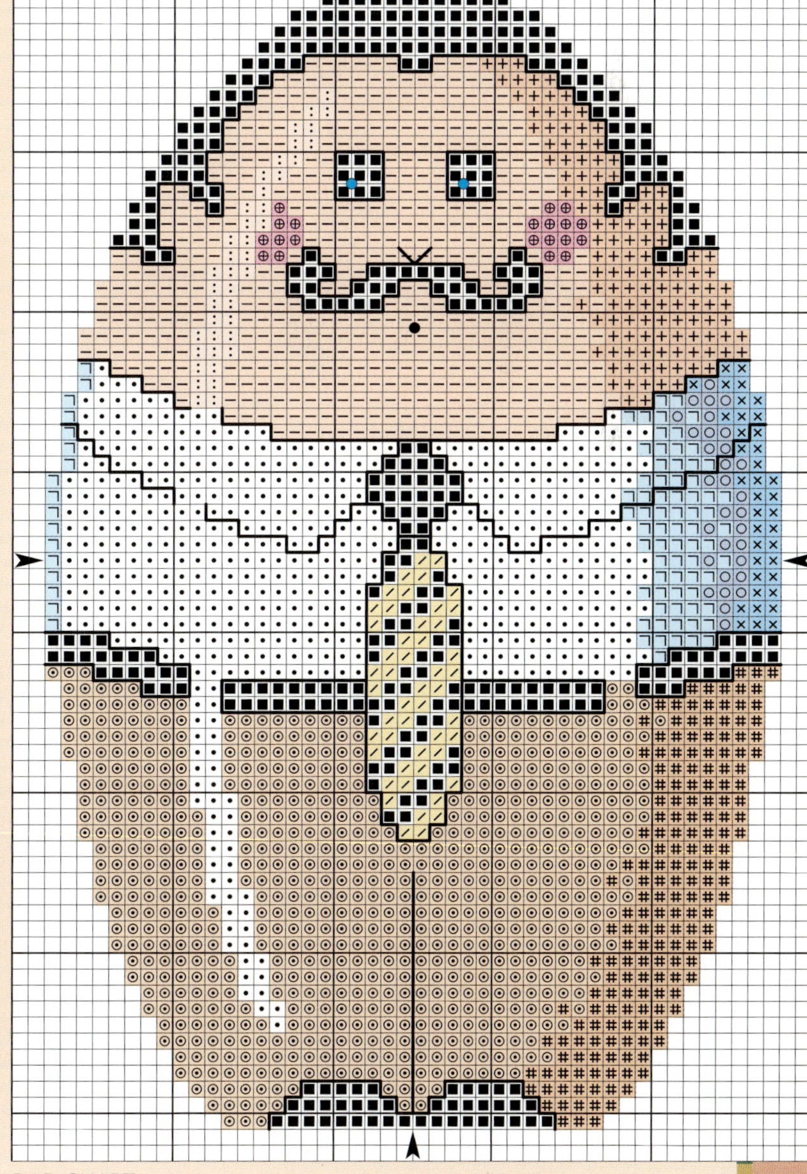

DAD CHART

ADORABLE DUCKY

As sweet as a vintage pull toy, this little quacker is just like the one Mary drew for Santa's sack! Crafted from wood shapes, he's been painted and trimmed in the colors kids love.

WHAT YOU'LL NEED

Acrylic paints in yellow, orange, red, bright blue, and black
Paintbrush
Wood egg
Two 1-inch-diameter wood balls
Tracing paper; pencil
⅛-inch-thick wood
Jigsaw
Fine sandpaper; tack cloth
Hot-glue gun and glue sticks
1½-inch wood ring
Scrap of bright blue felt
White fabric paint pen
Drill and ⅛-inch drill bit
2-inch-long piece of heavy crafts wire
Two red and one yellow wood beads
White oven-hardening clay, such as Sculpey
Toothpick; thick white crafts glue
6-inch-long piece of ⅛-inch-wide orange satin ribbon

HERE'S HOW

1 Paint the egg and one of the wood balls yellow. Shade the bottoms with orange if desired. Let the paint dry. To make the dots on the egg shape, dip the handle end of a paintbrush into red paint, and carefully dot onto the surface. Let the paint dry.

2 Trace the beak, tail, and foot patterns, *right*. Transfer to wood, and cut out. Sand the edges until smooth. Wipe away dust with a tack cloth. Paint the pieces with orange. Add yellow highlights if desired. Let dry.

3 Cut the remaining wood ball in half. Glue one half to the wood ring. Let dry. Paint with bright blue. Add white highlights if desired. Let dry.

4 Trace the collar pattern. Transfer to blue felt, and cut out. Use white fabric paint pen to create a line detail, placing it ⅛ inch from the collar edge. Let the paint dry.

5 Drill a hole in the bottom of the head piece, and in the top of the wood egg as shown, *opposite*. Glue one end of the wire piece into the hole in the egg. Slide on the blue felt collar, a red bead, a yellow bead, and another red bead. Glue the yellow-painted ball on the end of the wire. Let dry.

6 Glue the blue hat onto the head. Let dry.

7 For eyes, form two pea-size balls from clay. Bake in oven following the manufacturer's instructions. Let cool.

8 Arrange the painted feet side by side, and glue together. Let dry. Balance the duck's body on the feet, and glue in place. Let dry.

9 Glue on the beak and tail. Let dry. Glue the eyes onto the head where indicated. Let dry. To make the eye pupils, dip a toothpick into black paint, and dot the center of each eye. Let the paint dry.

10 Cut a 3×¼-inch piece of blue felt. Tie a knot in the center. Trim ends to make a bow tie. Use crafts glue to attach tie to neck and orange ribbon above the hat brim. Let dry.

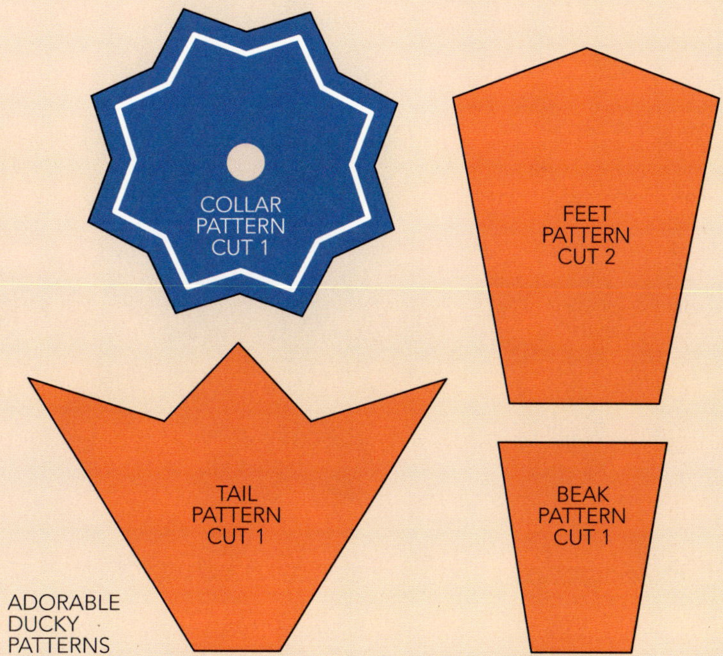

ADORABLE DUCKY PATTERNS

PLAYFUL BORDER TREE MAT

Re-creating the border on Mary's card, our bold tree mat is easily adaptable to different sizes. This mat measures 36 inches in diameter.

WHAT YOU'LL NEED

36-inch circle of black felt
33-inch circle of blue felt
27-inch circle of red felt
2¾ yards of black/white purchased piping or 2¾ yards piping cord plus ¼ yard black-and-white stripe fabric to make piping
Tracing paper; pencil
25-inch circle of gold felt, plus a 10×12-inch piece for stars
¼ yard of green felt
10×12-inch piece of pink felt
⅛ yard of white felt
Cotton embroidery floss in gold, green, red, and white; needle
64 small red pony beads
48 red 8mm faceted beads
87 white 8mm pearl beads
Fabric glue

HERE'S HOW

1 Center and layer the blue felt circle onto the black felt circle. Topstitch together. Center and layer red felt circle onto blue felt circle. Sandwich the raw edges of the black-and-white piping between the red and blue felt. Topstitch together. Trim the edge of the gold felt circle to have a rounded scallop. Center and layer the gold felt circle onto the red circle. Topstitch together.

2 Trace patterns, *below,* onto tracing paper.

3 For stem, cut a strip ½-inch wide × 2½ yards of green felt. Press stem into curved shape, and topstitch over raw edge of gold curved edge.

4 Use the patterns to cut the following:
58 green leaves for vine
16 green holly leaves
8 pink hearts
8 gold stars
66 white border rectangles

5 Attach the leaves to the stem according to the placement diagram, *page 179.* Use two plies of green floss to backstitch through the center. Arrange the stars, hearts, and holly leaves according to the placement diagram. Attach stars with two plies of gold floss and blanket stitches. Attach the holly leaves with seven French knots, *page 190,* for each leaf, with three plies of floss wrapped four times. Attach hearts with eight small red pony beads using two plies of red floss.

Use two plies of red floss to sew on red faceted beads around hearts. Use two plies of white floss to attach white pearls between leaves.

6 Glue white felt border pieces around the outside edge of the black circle.

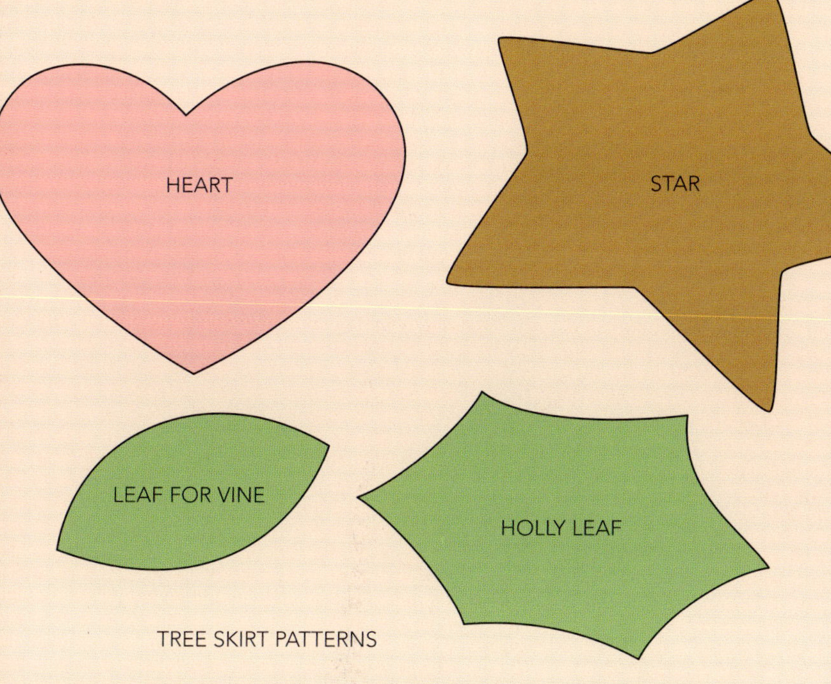

TREE SKIRT PATTERNS

PLAYFUL BORDER TREE MAT *continued*

PLAYFUL BORDER TREE MAT PATTERN

PLAYFUL BORDER TREE MAT PLACEMENT DIAGRAM

GIDDYAP STICK HORSE

All your little cowpokes will love finding Mary's ready-to-ride pony under the tree.

WHAT YOU'LL NEED

Tracing paper
Pencil
Scissors
8½×10-inch piece of 1½-inch-thick wood
Jigsaw
Sandpaper
Drill and 1-inch bit
36-inch-long piece of 1-inch dowel
2 plastic foam balls, such as Styrofoam, in 3½- and 4½-inch diameters
Sharp knife
Thick white crafts glue
½ yard of yellow fleece fabric
Straight pins
30-inch-long piece of blue cording for mane
Matching blue thread and hand sewing needle
30 inches of blue rickrack
Small red beads
Two 1-inch black buttons
Two 2-inch blue buttons
Yellow thread
1 yard of 1-inch-wide red braid trim
2 star-shaped buttons
Acrylic paints in lime and grass green
Paintbrush
1-inch-wide masking tape
30 inch piece of red ribbon

HERE'S HOW

1 Trace the horse head pattern, *page 183*, onto tracing paper. Use the pattern to transfer to 1½-inch-thick wood. Cut out and sand the edges. Wipe off dust.

2 Drill a hole into the bottom of the head where the stick will go. Drill in about 4 inches deep and 1 inch in diameter to accommodate the dowel.

3 Use a sharp knife to cut the plastic foam balls in half, making each side the same size.

4 Glue the smaller ball halves on each side of the nose, lining up the edge of the ball with the curve of the wood. Glue the large ball halves, lining up the edge with the back of the head.

5 Enlarge and transfer the head and ear patterns, *pages 182–183,* for yellow fabric onto tracing paper. Cut out and pin the pattern onto yellow fleece fabric. Cut out all pieces.

6 Pin the right sides of fabric together. Insert blue cording into the seam at the points marked on the pattern. Leave the loose extra length of blue cording inside the yellow fabric, and sew each end into the seam. Complete sewing both sides together, leaving an opening on the bottom. Turn the pieces right side out. The blue cording should be sewn into the seams on each end with a large loose piece in between. Shape the loose piece of blue cording into even loops between each end, pinning in place. Sew the cording in place firmly along the outside seam with a hand sewing needle and thread.

7 Sew each ear in the same manner, right sides together, leaving the bottom edge open. Fold a ½-inch hem inward on the bottom opening of the ear, and topstitch each ear closed

along the bottom edge. With hand sewing needle and thread, sew gathers along the bottom edge of ears. Sew onto the head with a hand sewing needle. Refer to the pattern for placement on the yellow head piece.

8 Sew blue rickrack along the bottom edge of the horse's head. Trim off the excess rickrack. Clip threads.

9 Sew beads, eyes, and nose onto yellow fabric, referring to pattern for placement. Position the yellow fabric headpiece on the wooden head base.

10 Cut a length of red braid to fit around the nose, and hand-stitch in place. Cut another

(continued on page 182)

GIDDYAP STICK HORSE *continued*

piece, and sew it onto the piece around the nose, bringing braid around the back of the head to complete the bridle. Sew a star onto each side of bridle.

11 Paint the wood dowel lime green. Let the paint dry. Beginning at one end of the dowel, wrap tape at an angle continuously downward. Press the tape firmly onto the dowel.

12 Paint the remaining dowel darker green, using the tape as a mask. Let the paint dry. Carefully remove the tape from the dowel.

13 Insert and glue the painted dowel into the hole in the wood head piece. Let the glue dry.

14 Tie a red ribbon around the neck. Trim the ribbon ends if necessary.

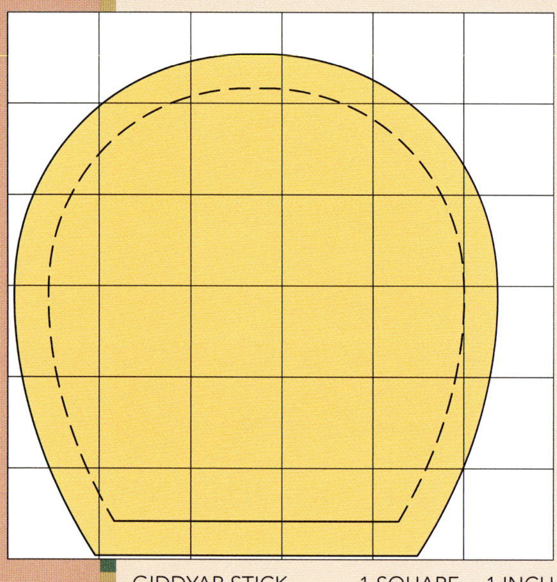

GIDDYAP STICK HORSE EAR PATTERN

1 SQUARE = 1 INCH

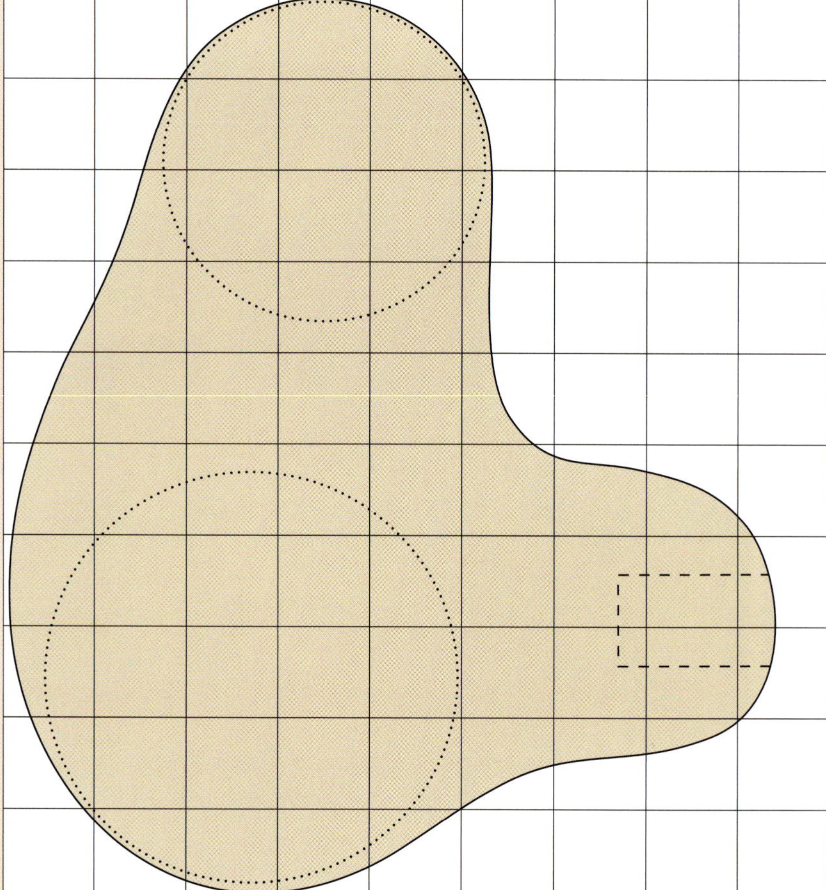

GIDDYAP STICK HORSE WOOD HEAD PATTERN

1 SQUARE = 1 INCH

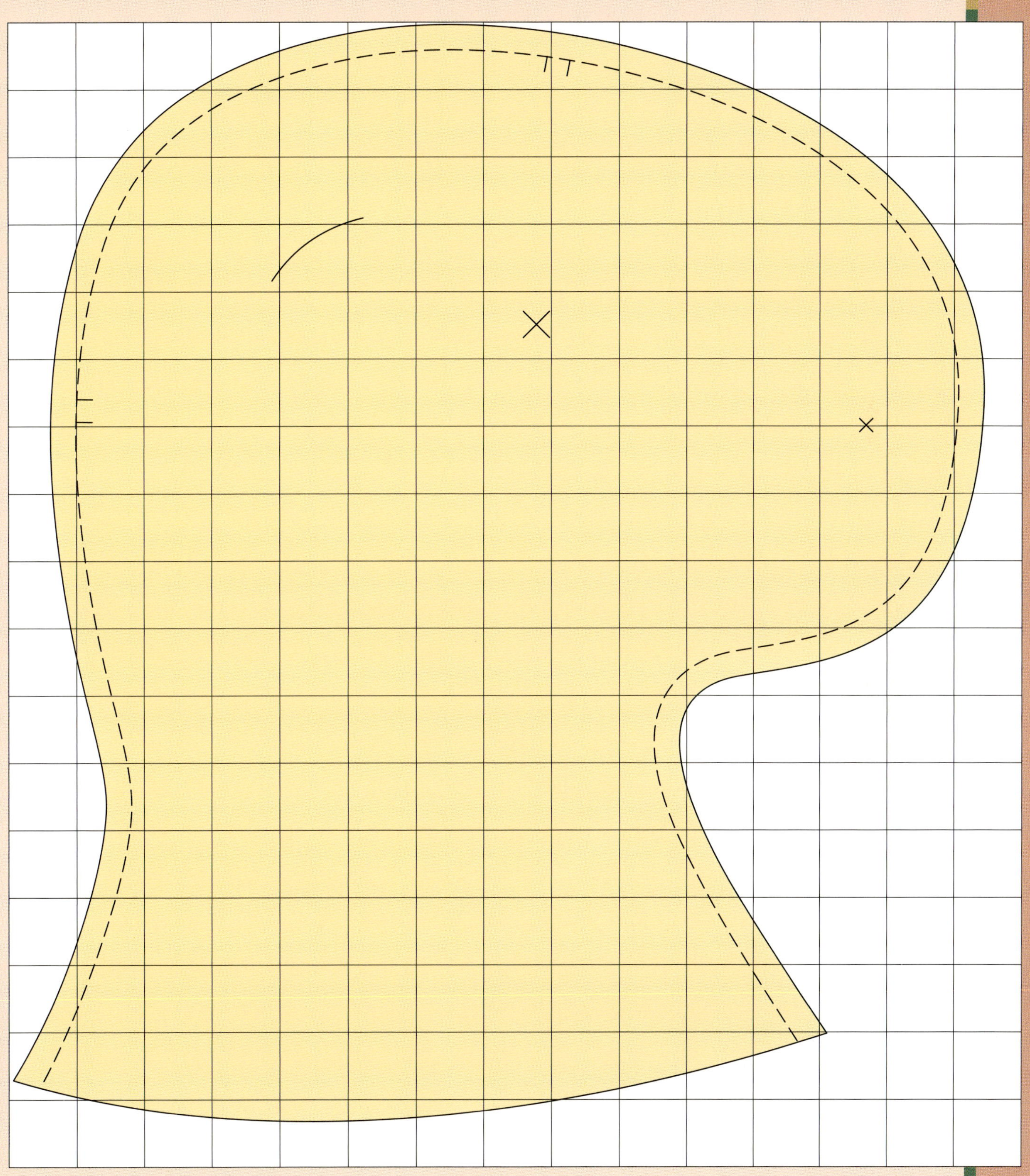

GIDDYAP STICK HORSE HEAD PATTERN

1 SQUARE = 1 INCH

NIGHT BEFORE CHRISTMAS PILLOW

Cross-stitched packages add the feeling of celebration to this keepsake holiday pillow that duplicates the border and saying on Mary's card.

WHAT YOU'LL NEED

12×18-inch piece of 20-count blue evenweave fabric
Cotton embroidery floss as listed in key; embroidery hoop; needle
1½ yards of red color corduroy fabric
Fusible interfacing
2 yards of sew-in red satin metallic twist piping
4 yards of tiny piping cord
4 yards of ¼-inch-wide gold trim
Fiberfil batting

HERE'S HOW

1 Tape or zigzag edges of fabric. Find center of chart, *pages 186–187,* and of fabric; begin stitching there. Use two plies of floss to work cross-stitches over

Anchor	DMC
002	000 White
403	310 Black
013	349 Dark coral
010	351 Light coral
075	604 Cranberry
256	704 Chartreuse
326	720 Bittersweet
295	726 Topaz
304	741 Medium tangerine
303	742 Light tangerine
1044	895 Hunter green
258	904 Deep parrot green
255	907 Light parrot green
1010	951 Ivory
039	961 Rose-pink
244	987 Forest green
410	995 Dark electric blue
433	996 Light electric blue
869	3743 Antique violet
167	3766 Peacock blue
386	3823 Yellow
1006	3831 Raspberry

BLENDED NEEDLE

1005 9046	816 Light garnet (1X) and 321 Christmas red (1X)
897 896	902 Deep garnet (1X) and 3857 Rosewood (1X)

BACKSTITCH

002	000 White – gift boxes on top of lettering (2X)
403	310 Black – all remaining stitches (2X)
683	500 Blue-green – holly leaf veins (2X)
075	604 Cranberry – gift box in lower left corner (2X)
256	704 Chartreuse – holly leaves (2X)
326	720 Bittersweet – lettering (3X)
295	726 Topaz – lettering (3X)
304	741 Medium tangerine – lettering (3X)
1005	816 Light garnet – ribbon on gift box in lower left corner, stars on gift box in lower right corner (2X)
258	904 Deep parrot green – hearts on gift box in lower left corner (2X)
244	987 Forest green – gift bags, gift box on right side (2X)

STRAIGHT STITCH

1005	816 Light garnet – gift box in upper left corner (2X)
244	987 Forest green – gift box in upper left corner (2X)

FRENCH KNOT

403	310 Black – gift bags
304	741 Medium tangerine – lettering and gift box in lower left corner
258	904 Deep parrot green – gift box in lower left corner
244	987 Forest green – gift box in lower right corner

SURFACE ATTACHMENTS

122 Beadery Red pearl beads
135 Beadery White pearl beads
689 Beadery Gold 15mm stars

Stitch count: *90 high x 165 wide*

Finished design sizes:
20-count fabric – 9 x 16½ inches
28-count fabric – 6½ x 11¾ inches
32-count fabric – 5⅝ x 10⅜ inches

two threads of fabric. Work French knots, *page 190*, using two plies. Work the remainder of stitches as noted in key.

2 Press the finished piece from the back. Attach beads and buttons using two plies of floss.

3 Stitch seams with right sides together using ¼-inch seams. Cut four 1½-inch-wide sashing strips from corduroy: two 15 inches long and two 23 inches long. Fuse interfacing to wrong side. Stitch strips next to cross-stitch, mitering corners. Trim excess. Stitch piping around edge.

4 Cut the pillow back the same size as the front. Fuse the interfacing to the wrong side.

5 Cut a ruffle 4½-inches-wide by 1½ times the fullness of pillow. Piece the short ends as necessary. Press ruffle in half lengthwise, wrong sides facing.

6 Position tiny piping cord inside ruffle at pressed edge. Topstitch gold trim next to piping on front side of ruffle. Gather raw edges, and stitch ruffle to piping. Stitch pillow front to back leaving an opening for turning. Trim corners. Turn to the right side.

7 Add batting to the inside of the pillow. Stitch the opening closed.

NIGHT BEFORE CHRISTMAS PILLOW *continued*

INDEX

PAGE 12

PAGE 88

PAGE 80

PAGE 164

STITCHING DIAGRAMS

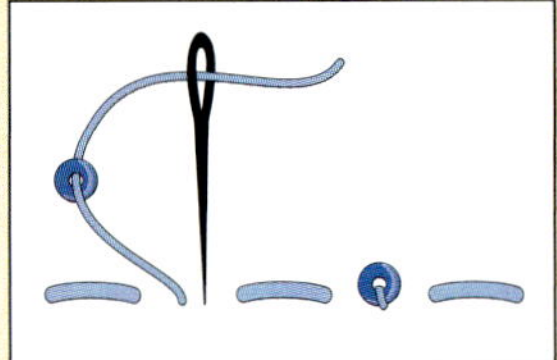
ADDING BEADS

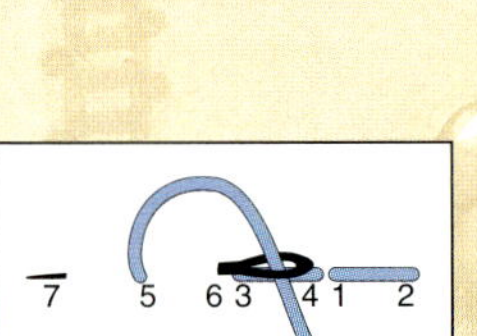

BACKSTITCH

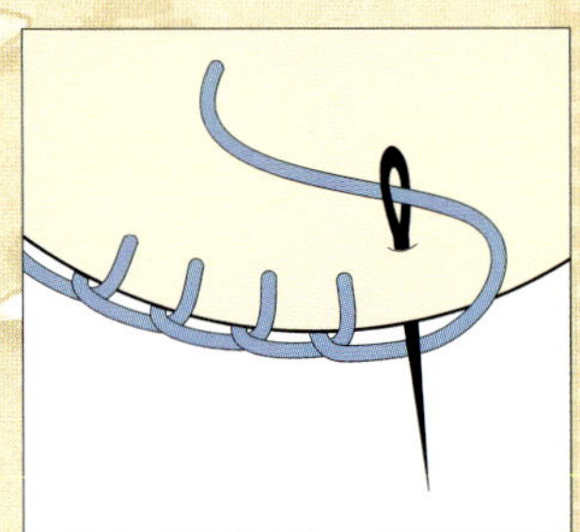
BLANKET STITCH

CHAIN STITCH

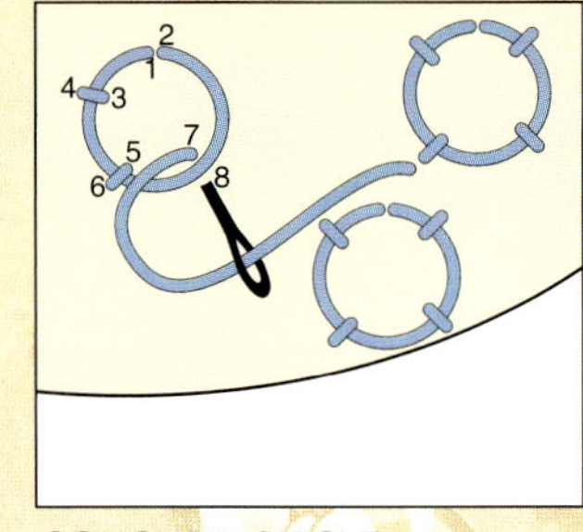

COUCHED CIRCLE

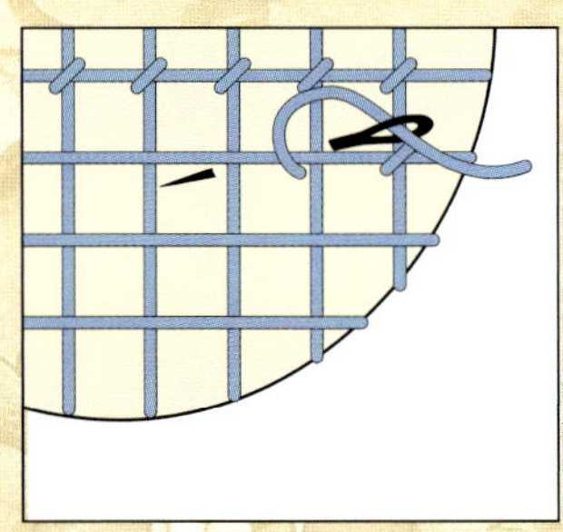
COUCHED PLAID

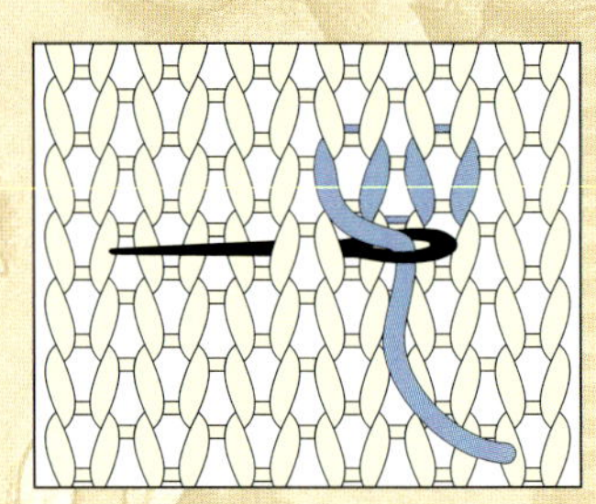
DUPLICATE STITCH

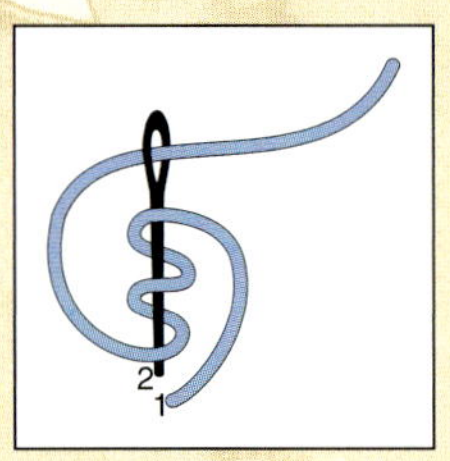

FRENCH KNOT

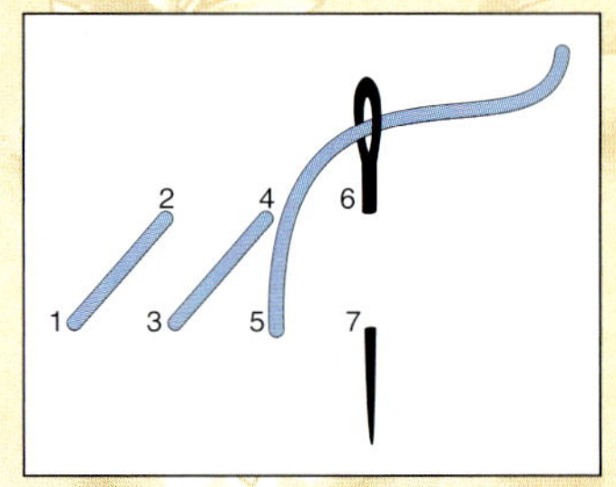

HALF-CROSS-STITCH

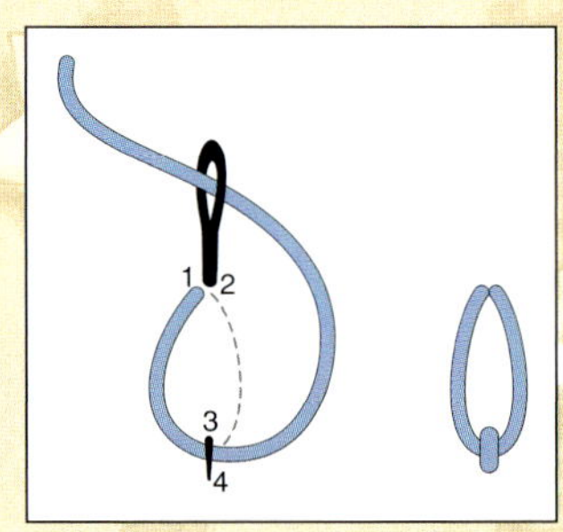

LAZY DAISY

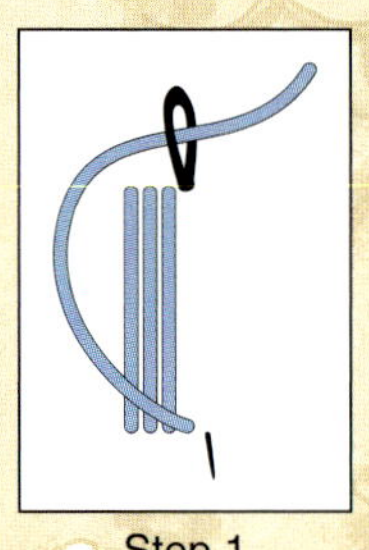
Step 1

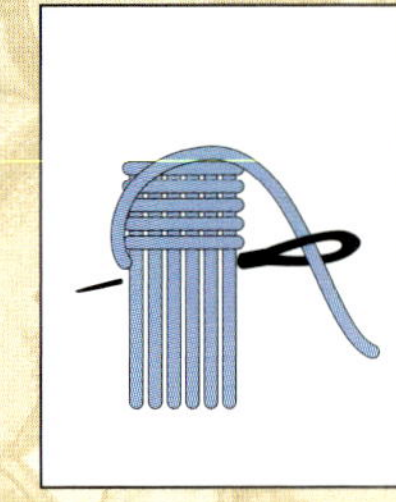
Step 2

PADDED SATIN STITCH

Knitting Abbreviations

Beg - beginning
BO - bind off
CO - cast on
Cont - continue
Dec - decrease
Dpn - double pointed needles
Est - established
Inc - increase
K - knit
K2tog - knit next two stitches together
MB - make bobble
P - purl
Pat - pattern
Rem - remaining
Rep - repeat
Rnd(s) - round; rounds
RS - right side
St st - stockinette stitch
St(s) - stitch; stitches
WS - wrong side
Yb - yarn back
Yo - yarn over

Crochet Abbreviations

Beg - beginning
Bet - between
Ch - chain
Dec - decrease
Est - established
Inc - increase
Hk - hook
Lp(s) - loop; loops
Rem - remaining
Rep - repeat
Rnd(s) - round; rounds
RS - right side
Sc - single crochet
Sc2tog - single crochet the next two stitches together
Sl st - slip stitch
St(s) - stitch; stitches
Yo - yarn over

SOURCES

Designers
Susan Banker
Barbara Sestock
Margaret Sindelar
Anne Smith
Alice Wetzel

Cross-Stitchers
Diana Dusing
Karen Eis
Nancy Eis
Vicki Jacobs
Carla Johnson
Colleen Johnson
Gail Kimel
Carolyn Knittle
Beth Sherman

Models
Elizabeth Dahlstrom
Krista DeJong
Riley Jones
Sarah Ramundt
Clarissa Ann Tusa
Jack Tusa

Photographers
Scott Little
Andy Lyons

Photostyling
Carol Dahlstrom
Donna Chesnut, Assistant

Product Sources
Cross-Stitch Fabric
Zweigart
262 Old New Brunswick Road
Piscataway, NJ 08854
908/271-1949

Embroidery Floss
Anchor
Consumer Service Department
P.O. Box 27067
Greenville, SC 29616

DMC
Port Kearney Building 10
South Kearney, NJ
07032-0650

Ribbon
CM Offray & Son Inc.
Route 24, Box 601
Chester, NJ 07930-0601
908/879-4700

Sewing Machine
Viking #1 Plus
Husqvarna Viking Sewing Machines
31000 Viking Parkway
Westlake, OH 44145
440/808-6550

Wool Felt
National Non Wovens
www.nationalnonwovens.com
sales@nationalnonwovens.com